Trains

East Anglia

C000174165

Contents

About the book

Whoever said that writing a second book is more difficult than writing the first one was certainly not wrong! After several gigabytes of e-mails and file transfers and scanning, combined with about 600 miles of driving, the book has finally fallen into place. It has been a lot of fun visiting old haunts that I remember from childhood. And whilst the sight, 30 years ago, of triple headed 37s on what were then called 'Freightliners' will never fade from my memory it was equally impressive watching the first run of a single class 70 'Powerhaul' effortlessly lifting 30 wagons out of Felixstowe dock.

The Anglia region has always seen a wide range of traction and train variety, but some of the locations in the book have not changed significantly since the railway arrived.

I never thought a book could be delayed by the 'wrong type of snow' but the freak snow of Christmas 2009 made getting around Norfolk a little 'difficult' but as you can see we got there in the end.

Marcus Dawson
Hertfordshire
February 2010

HOW DOES THE BOOK WORK?

Chapter Information
Gives information about the traffic flows for the section of line covered. However, these are subject to change without notice and should be used as a guide only (especially freight workings).

Location Notes
Gives general information about the area - the surroundings, the amount of road traffic, the type of people likely to be encountered, whether wellingtons will be needed.

Public Transport
Since not everyone has a car, these notes give information on using public transport.
All public transport information is correct at the time of writing. Walking times are given as a guide only.
Bus services and frequencies shown apply to Monday to Friday daytimes only. Weekend and evening services may be different or non existent.

Bus routes and times can change at short notice so please always check before travelling.
Recommended public transport planning tools are:
http://www.travelineeastanglia.org.uk
http://www.nationalrail.co.uk   http://www.transportdirect.info
http://www.taxiregister.com   or you can telephone Traveline on 0871 200 2233.
The destination bus stop, where it is not close to the location is indicated by a **B**

Amenities
Gives information on toilets, places to eat and other local facilities that can be reached easily from the location.

Accommodation
Gives information on places to stay nearby, if any.

Photographic Notes
Gives information on the times of day* that provide the best light conditions, the height of the bridge parapet, whether a step ladder be useful, whether there is enough room to stand and for a video tripod. What sources of noise would interfere with audio recordings.

Each picture contains details of the time, month and lens so the photographer can plan ahead. In order to make this book, each location has been revisited and checked within the last 2 months and the pictures are representative of the current shot available. If there are any changes they have been noted in the text.

Any times quoted represent the summer months when the sun rises early and sets in the late evening. These should be taken as a guide as the sun will rise or set outside these times during certain months of year.

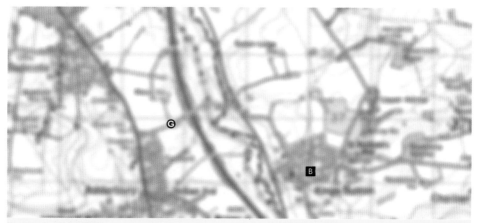

Postcode: X00 0XX   **Lat N00:00:00**   **Long W00:00:00**

Sat Nav information and Road directions

The postcode provides a reference for your Satellite Navigation system. This will take you to the place indicated by the **G** on the map which will be close to the location. If it is not on the location, use the map for the last few yards. These post codes did not include house numbers so if a house number is requested, please ignore it. They were checked using a 2010 Garmin Nuvi system. Other systems should provide similar results.

The location is always at the centre of the map and the Latitude and Longitude provide an absolute reference to this point. The map squares represent a 1 kilometre scale, which is approximately two-thirds of a mile.

Acknowledgements

This book would not have been possible with out help and original input from:

David Beardmore, Jonathan Benton, Chris Boon, Scott Borthwick, Ian Bowskill, Jon Bradley, Robert Brooks, Ben Cannell, Ken Carr, Ron Carr, Brian Carter, Jonathan Cordle, Michael Davis, Paul Davis, Albert Dawson, David Dawson, Peter Foster, Robert Gooding, Steve Goodrum, Calum Hepplewhite, John Hooson, Mark Ireland, Tom Jenkins, Chris Nesbitt, Steve Philpott, Sarah Power, Michael Proudfoot, Luke Putland, Allan Sibley, Nick Slocombe, David Smith, Michael Smith, Oli Smith, Ewan Tait, Richard Tearle, Geoff Tibble, John Tomlinson, James Welham, Ben Wheeler and the Anglia Gen Group.

Important Note

Advice about the general environment of each location is given on each page. This information is a guide only. Always be careful. Avoid leaving your property on display and be aware of your surroundings at all times. There are, sadly, people who will not think twice about trying to steal your equipment.

Visions International Entertainment Ltd does not condone trespass and none of the information in this book should be taken as a right to trespass.

The information in this book has been published in good faith by Visions International Entertainment Ltd. All liability for loss, disappointment, negligence or damage caused by reliance on the information in this book is hereby excluded to the fullest extent permitted by law.

'East Suffolk' and 'Wherry' Lines

General Notes

The line from Lowestoft to Ipswich, or Oulton Broad South to Westerfield to be precise, is signalled by the Radio Electronic Token Block (RETB) so any unit or locomotive using the line needs to be suitably equipped for this.

If anyone is in possession of the right piece of radio equipment then all the RETB activity on the East Suffolk line can be monitored on either 205.15, 205.65 or 205.90 Mhz.

When driving around the area it is probably worth noting that the Reedham Ferry is not always a useful short cut. Although the crossing of the river is a minute or two you can sometimes have to wait in a queue of traffic to board the ferry. If you are in a hurry it might be best to avoid the ferry altogether and take the longer road route.

1) 156417 on the bend towards Reedham Junction.
Photo by Albert Dawson, May, 11:00, 55mm

Passenger Traffic

The line is worked by the Norwich Crown Point fleet of either 153s, 156s or 170s units.

Freight Traffic

There is no freight traffic booked along the lines.

Occasional Traffic

The line hosts a number of workings that could be classed as occasional but tend to happen every year! There are 'The Drags', usually during a section of the summer timetable, where a London to Norwich working is extended out to Great Yarmouth. This requires the use of diesel traction dragging the MkIII set, complete with 90 and DVT, out to the coast. These workings can run via either Reedham or Acle, check the local Anglia Gen Group for details (http://finance. groups.yahoo.com/group/anglia-gen).

Another yearly occurrence is the 'Lowestoft Seafront Air Festival' specials, usually on a Thursday and Friday during the school summer holidays. These usually consist of the spare MkIII set from Norwich Crown Point top and tailed with class 47s, for ease of reversal in Lowestoft Station.

In the autumn there are also the Rail Head Treatment Trains, in the past these have been worked by DRS from their Stowmarket base and can produce pretty much any class from their traction fleet.

2) 20305 and 20306 pass Haddiscoe bound for Lowestoft.
Photo by Brian Carter, August, 11:15, 85mm

3) 70013 passes Weston heading south to Ipswich.
Photo by Michael Smith, May, 09:00, 325mm

'East Suffolk' and 'Wherry' Lines

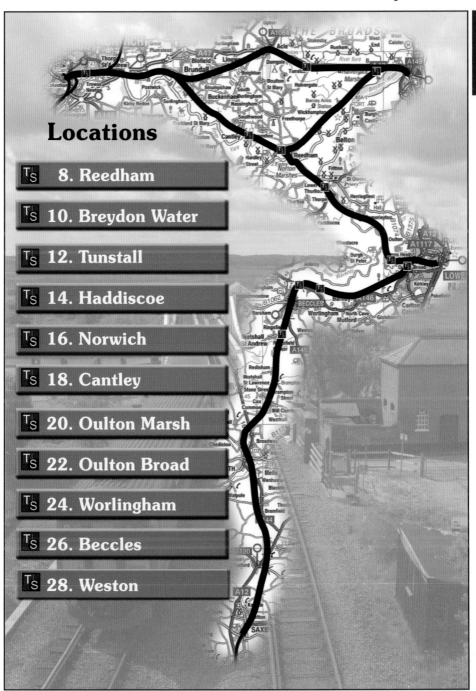

Locations

T|S	8. Reedham
T|S	10. Breydon Water
T|S	12. Tunstall
T|S	14. Haddiscoe
T|S	16. Norwich
T|S	18. Cantley
T|S	20. Oulton Marsh
T|S	22. Oulton Broad
T|S	24. Worlingham
T|S	26. Beccles
T|S	28. Weston

Reedham

Location Notes
The locations are two road bridges over the railway on the edge of Reedham village. The junction is where the line splits to either Great Yarmouth or Lowestoft. The Swing Bridge is where the Lowestoft line crosses the River Yare.

Public Transport
From Reedham station: exit the station, head south down Station Road and continue on this road when it changes to The Hills. When you reach the crossroads with Mill Road turn left to reach the junction, or right to reach the river front or straight on to get to the road bridge that overlooks the swing bridge.

Amenities
There are two small shops in Reedham village, one of which is a general store on The Hills. This is open from 08:30 to 22:00. Next door there is a chip shop which is open Thursday to Saturday.

Pettitts Animal Adventure Park, on the edge of the village, could provide a good 'family' place to go between workings.

The Ship public house is situated next to the Swing Bridge, and its beer garden may also offer a shot! There are public toilets opposite The Ship.

The CAMRA Good Beer Guide listed the Railway Tavern, by the station, as serving good food and real ale. There is also the Humpty Dumpty Brewery on Church Road, which has an off-licence shop.

1) 47714 tails a Norwich working across the junction.
Photo by Albert Dawson, September, 14:45, 300mm

Accommodation
There are two Bed and Breakfasts in Reedham Village: The Railway Tavern by the station - 01493 700340 and The Horseshoe: 01493 700140.

Photographic Notes
Both of these locations can be popular so if there is a special working expect a few people! Both roads are very quiet so videographers would suffer more from other photographers than traffic noise.

The Great Yarmouth line has a 20mph limit across the bridge and all the signals in the area are semaphores, so trains will be moving slowly.

For the Swing Bridge the best shot is looking south from the road bridge, of a train crossing the swing bridge, ideally coming from Lowestoft. The shot of a Lowestoft bound train is uninspiring.

The shot from the quayside, of trains crossing the swing bridge, is pretty much side-on. There are options on both the east and west sides, although the bridge itself and the signal box, which is in the middle of the bridge on the west side, will obscure part of the train.

From the junction the best shots are of trains coming off the Great Yarmouth (Berney Arms) line, so

2) 47832 pauses as 156419 heads towards Norwich.
Photo by Richard Tearle, September, 16:15, 70mm

looking east. There is a semaphore, albeit behind a sighting board, in this shot.

The parapet of the junction bridge is high so a step ladder is essential; and space can be quite tight when the location is busy.

Reedham

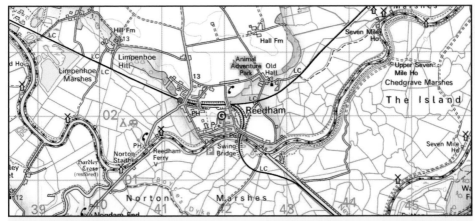

Postcode: NR13 3UF   **Lat N52:33:43**   **Long W01:34:14**

Road Directions

Taking the A47 from Norwich, leave at the B1140 junction, the road splits either side of a central reservation before the junction. but turn right at the roundabout (over the railway line, past the station) rather than going into the village. Follow the B1140 through Freethorpe. If approaching from Great Yarmouth on the A47 turn left at the Stracey Arms onto an unclassified road which goes over the parallel railway line, and follow this road through Halvergate towards Freethorpe on the B1140. At the edge of Reedham, near the start of the 30mph limit and the village sign, turn left, signed 'Zoo', then take the 2nd right. The bridge is about ¼ of a mile further on. Both locations are on narrow roads, there are places to park near the location but it would be better to park in the village and walk a few yards to the locations.

3) With river traffic passing beneath, 20096 & 906 cross River Yare Swing Bridge with an ACORP special to Norwich.
Photo by Albert Dawson, September, 13:00, 120mm

Breydon Water

Location Notes

This is a small embankment on the Wherryman's Way footpath. Bordering the Acle Marshes, it is also within the Breydon Nature Reserve. There will be walkers and bird watchers around. As there is no lighting in the area the location is not a lot of use after dark.

1) 47832, with the Yarmouth wind farm in the background and a 33103 on the tail, takes the Acle line to Norwich.
   Photo by Albert Dawson, September, 12:45, 300mm

Public Transport

The location is about 10 minutes walk from Great Yarmouth station, via the footpath from the bridge corner of the Asda car park.

Amenities

There is the large Asda by the station and the town has everything else you might need.

Accommodation

Great Yarmouth is a prime Norfolk holiday destination, there are numerous hotels and guest houses in the town.

Photographic Notes

The location is an embankment that is there to strengthen the bank against the tide. You are raised up well above platform height. Trains to Norwich are heading south west so the light would favour afternoon

2) Heading into Great Yarmouth 47810 on a drag with 90003.
   Photo by Albert Dawson, July, 12:45, 130mm

shots. For workings heading to Great Yarmouth a very early morning view will catch the light. You will also see workings heading via Acle but the location is too close to the junction for you to change to that line in time to get a close shot.

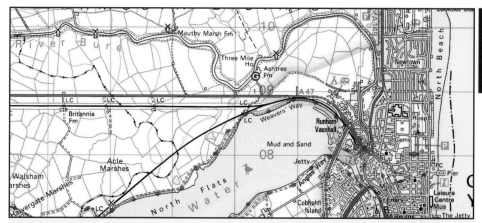

Postcode: NR30 1TD   **Lat N52:37:04**   **Long W01:41:36**

Road Directions

Approaching Great Yarmouth on the A47, the location is off a lay-by just before you enter the town.
If approaching on the A12 from the south continue all the way through Great Yarmouth, crossing over the river bridge. At the roundabout take the first exit and continue on the A47. You will see the railway line on your left. After about ¾ of a mile you will see the footpath lay-by.

3) 47832 powers away from Great Yarmouth, taking the Reedham line, with a working bound for London.
Photo by David Dawson, August, 10:15, 60mm

Tunstall, Stracey Arms

Location Notes

Located about 3 miles west of Great Yarmouth on the line to Norwich this location is a road bridge. It is named after one of the previous incarnations of the Pontiac Road House pub, which used to be a restaurant, but is, at the time of writing, up for sale.

1) 47832, with 90005 dead in tow, slows on the approach to Great Yarmouth with a service from Liverpool Street.
Photo by David Dawson, August, 14:45, 80mm

Public Transport

Anglian Bus and Coach, service A47, operates from Great Yarmouth, Station Road to the Stracey Arms stop which is opposite the location.

Amenities

As the restaurant is closed, the nearest amenities are in Great Yarmouth which has a large Asda supermarket just opposite the station.

Accommodation

Great Yarmouth has a wide range of hotels and guest houses.

Photographic Notes

The line approaching from the Great Yarmouth direction is straight until just before the location where it curves round, providing a view with the Stracey Windmill in the background.

For trains heading towards Great Yarmouth the line is straight for a mile or so heading in a south east direction towards the locaiton.

The only source of noise is the nearby A47, but the bridge is in open countryside and will be very windy on all but a still day.

The flat nature of the land around the bridge provides an excellent view of the line and the open countryside for many miles around. However, this also means the bridge is very exposed to the elements.

Tunstall, Stracey Arms

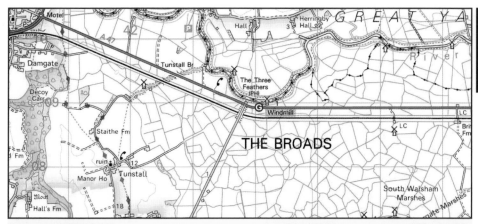

Postcode: NR13 3QE   **Lat N52:37:21**   **Long W01:36:00**

Road Directions

Take the A47 from Norwich and follow the signs towards Great Yarmouth. After the roundabout leaving Acle, continue for about a mile along the A47 and you will see the restaurant site on the left.

Park in the restaurant car park. Do not drive down Branch Road as there is nowhere to park on the southern side of the bridge for some considerable distance.

2) DRS traction stepping in to lend a hand as 20304 tops with 47712 en route to Norwich, substituting for a failed 156.
Photo by Steve Goodrum, February, 13:30, 45mm

Haddiscoe

Location Notes

This location is a major road bridge over the railway and river in the middle of the countryside. There are a few houses nearby and the village of St Olaves is just to the east.

1) 'Wherry Lines' 156422 follows the 'New Cut' of the Broads river Yare and heads towards Lowestoft.
   Photo by Albert Dawson, July, 10:30, 120mm

Public Transport

Local services from Norwich to Lowestoft call at Haddiscoe station but it is a request stop.
The local bus operator is Anglia Bus and Coach whose 577, 581 services operate from Great Yarmouth and pass through Haddiscoe.

Amenities

There are not many facilities in the immediate vicinity. There are some small shops in St. Olaves. Otherwise, the nearest facilities are in Great Yarmouth, Lowestoft or Norwich.

2) 47802 on a Norwich bound returning air show special.
   Photo by Albert Dawson, July, 11:00, 35mm

Photographic Notes

The line runs north east to south west. Shots are possible in both directions. These feature the river in the very flat marshy landscape.
Shots of workings heading towards Lowestoft are best lit from mid morning until mid afternoon after which the sun will come round for Summer Norwich bound workings.
The location offers some very good opportunities for both telephoto shots and video work as approaching trains can be seen for many miles from the bridge. Road noise will be a factor though and it is not possible to get a shot from both sides as the road is wide and there are crash barriers between the pavement and road.

3) Norwich bound 47802, seen from the approach road.
   Photo by Ben Wheeler, July, 16:15, 50mm

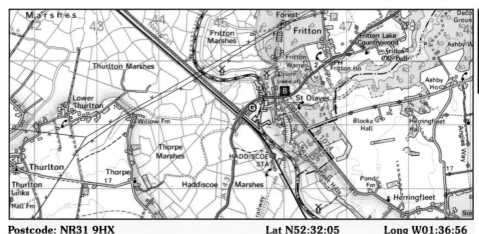

Postcode: NR31 9HX   **Lat N52:32:05**   **Long W01:36:56**

Road Directions

The location **is** the A143 bridge over the railway and the River Waveney, closer to the village of St. Olaves than Haddiscoe. The A143 runs south west from Great Yarmouth to Bury St Edmunds. If travelling from Lowestoft take the B1074 from Oulton, via Somerleyton to St. Olaves. In St Olaves turn left at the T junction and join the A143. Pass over the traffic light controlled river bridge and then the main bridge itself. Park on the grass verge of the station approach road, by the junction with the A143, south of the bridge and walk back up.

4) 20096 and 20906 lead 47714 bumbling back towards Norwich with the last train of the Norfolk ACORP weekend.
Photo by Ken Brunt, September, 15:30, 75mm

Norwich, Country Park

Location Notes
This location is within the Whitlingham Country Park, looking across the River Yare to the line. The original river course is the route that goes under the bridge and the 'New Cut' is the route for larger boats.
The park is just under 300 acres and has cycle paths and pathways for walkers. You are slightly off these, on embankments. Being open countryside there is little in the way of lighting to illuminate the scene across the river so there would be little point in being here after dark. But it is a quiet, relaxing place, aside from the odd jet ski or children's Pirate Ship on the lake.

1) With an ECS move to Lowestoft 47501 heads east. The last overhead mast can be seen behind the second coach.
Photo by Albert Dawson, July, 17:00, 100mm

Public Transport
Anglian Bus and Coach, service 587, runs from St Stephens Street to Trowse, May Gurney depot. There are connecting buses from Norwich Station to St Stephens, which is behind the main bus station.

Amenities
There is a picnic meadow and a visitors centre with a café, information point and toilet facilities.

Photographic Notes
Trains can be passing at a reasonable speed here, around 40mph and they appear from behind bushes in both directions. You can be fooled by the noise of approaching trains as you can also hear the main lines and shunting at Crown Point depot, which is just to the west of the location. Depending on your position you can go from water side to almost track height, but you will have to work around the trees and bushes on the riverside.

There is only the distant noise of Norwich, or sound of passing boats, so audio recordings should be clear from distractions.

2) 156416 heads into Norwich from Sheringham.
Photo by Albert Dawson, July, 09:15, 120mm

Norwich, Country Park

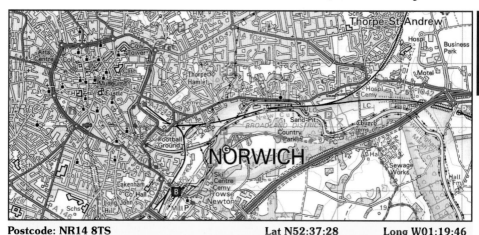

Postcode: NR14 8TS   **Lat N52:37:28**   **Long W01:19:46**

Road Directions

From the A47 (Norwich by pass section) take the A146 into Norwich. You will pass over both the Thetford and Great Eastern lines before reaching the A146/A1054 junction. Turn right and follow the A1054 Martineau Lane, past the BP Garage on your right and follow it to the next roundabout where you should take the fourth exit and follow this road, crossing over the railway and the River Yare. When you have gone under the power lines the road curves to the right, but you should turn left into Whittingham Lane. Follow this road until you reach the first pay and display car park. This is the best parking option as you can follow the footpath that divides the two lakes across to the Outdoor Education Centre from where you follow the footpath right to reach the location.

3) 47802 hauls a National Express MkIII set, with DVT 82127 at the front, back from Lowestoft in to Norwich.
Photo by Albert Dawson, July, 16:30, 35mm

Cantley

Location Notes

Cantley is in Norfolk about 6 miles east of Norwich. It is the location of the British Sugar factory, which was the first sugar beet factory in the UK. The location is at the end of a rural track between Limpenhoe and the Cantley Sugar factory. The dirt track is rarely used and the only people you are likely to encounter are walkers. After poor weather the track is very muddy.

1) 20096 and 20906, with an Anglian MkIII set, head south west towards Reedham Junction with an ACORP special.
Photo by Jonathan Cordle, September, 16:50, 75mm

Public Transport

National Express East Anglia operates a service to Cantley station from Norwich. Come out of the station and head into the village, taking the next right after the sugar factory entrance onto Grange Road and follow the footpath through the marshes to the location.

Amenities

The village has one pub, the Reedcutter, which is down a lane off Station Road.

Photographic Notes

The line is very straight through the location. From the foot crossing you can see for a couple of miles to the north west, well past Cantley Station. There is nothing to cast shadows, aside from the semaphore behind you. For shots of trains heading to Reedham the British Sugar factory will dominate the landscape.

2) 47832 tails a Lowestoft bound ACORP special.
Photo by Albert Dawson, September, 13:45, 35mm

Cantley

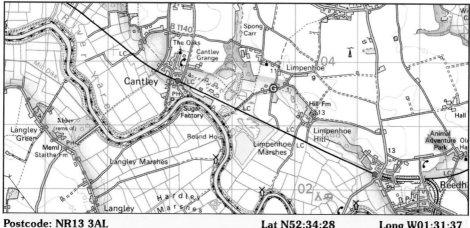

Postcode: NR13 3AL **Lat N52:34:28** **Long W01:31:37**

Road Directions

From the A47 heading towards Great Yarmouth, just after North Burlingham take the B1140 south towards Beighton and the continue, through Cucumber Corner, to Southwood and then Limpenhoe. Once in Limpenhoe turn onto Marsh Road and follow this road to the crossing.

3) Bagpipe Crompton 33103 passes the British Sugar factory with a Lowestoft bound working.
Photo by Albert Dawson, September, 13:45, 130mm

Lowestoft, Oulton Marsh

Location Notes
Situated on the western edge of Lowestoft this location is in open fields in the Norfolk Broads. The location is an unlit crossing on a footpath that leads to the broad. Although you could drive all the way to the location you would not get far on the other side unless you were in a tractor. In wet weather the path will be very muddy. The only people likely to be passing are walkers.

1) 156417 heads round the curve out of Lowestoft and onwards towards Reedham and Norwich.
   Photo by Albert Dawson, July, 11:45, 35mm

Public Transport
Ambassador Travel, service 606, operates hourly, calling at Oulton Broad, North Railway Station and then on to Oulton, Christmas Lane, from where it would be a 10 minute walk to the location.

Amenities
There is nothing at the location but Lowestoft has many shops.

Photographic Notes
The location offers a good view of workings approaching Lowestoft with the sun being good until early afternoon, after which it would be too far round. Wider views from along the lane are hindered by trees.

There is another crossing, at the other corner of the rail curve, that would be on until much later in the afternoon.

There is nothing in the area to generate noise, so apart from wind, there is little to spoil audio recordings.

2) Tailing a MkIII set 47802 is off to enjoy the Lowestoft Airshow.
   Photo by Albert Dawson, July, 12:30, 35mm

Lowestoft, Oulton Marsh

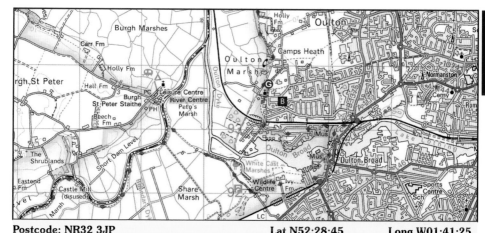

Postcode: NR32 3JP   **Lat N52:28:45**   **Long W01:41:25**

Road Directions

From the north take the A12 south from Great Yarmouth until you reach the roundabout where the B1375 splits off. Take the B1375 and cross over two more large roundabouts. Continue along until just before the third large roundabout where there is a mini roundabout and turn right onto Hall Road.

From the south, follow the A12 into Lowestoft and then take the A1117, straight on at the roundabout where the A12 continues right. Follow the road straight across two roundabouts and at the end turn right. Continue along the road and pass both Oulton Broad Stations. After the level crossing for Oulton Broad North continue across the roundabout and at the mini roundabout turn left onto Hall Road.

Follow Hall Road for about a mile, it bends round into Christmas Lane, and continue to the small roundabout at the end where you should turn left into Church Lane. Follow Church Lane to St Michaels Close on the left and park, considerately, around here.

Continuing on foot down Church Lane, walk down the dirt track and turn left at the bottom. This track will lead you to the location.

3) 47501 sweeps its way through the Oulton Marshes with a Lowestoft Airshow special.
Photo by Albert Dawson, July, 12:30, 60mm

Oulton Broad Swing Bridge

Location Notes
On the coast of Norfolk, Lowestoft is about 20 miles from Norwich. The bridge is opposite the lock between Lake Lothing, a salt water lake that forms Lowestoft Harbour, and the Oulton Fresh Water Broad.

1) A One Railway 170 crosses the bridge on its way south along the East Suffolk Line to Ipswich.
Photo by Chris Boon, May, 17:45, 40mm

Public Transport
You can take the train to Oulton Broad South Station and then walk back up Bridge Road and onto Saltwater Way. It will be safest to cross opposite the railway on Victoria Road as the A1117 can be quite busy.

Amenities
There are some shops on Bridge Road, including a pub, chip shop and Spar Store/Post Office.

Photographic Notes
Although shots are possible from the eastern side of the bridge these are all from private property, so the

2) From the waste ground, a sprinter heads south.
January, 15:00, 60mm

location will favour southbound afternoon trains. The A1117 has a large 'viewing area' as part of the bridge structure and the footpath under the bridge offers some height variations on the bridge. For shots of the bridge's southern side you can shoot over a wall. A step ladder would be handy, although not essential, as the wall is about 5 feet high and about a foot thick. The A1117 will be quite noisy which will affect video. There is limited scope for shots from the northern side of the bridge, this waste land is fenced off and may be redeveloped in the future.

Oulton Broad Swing Bridge

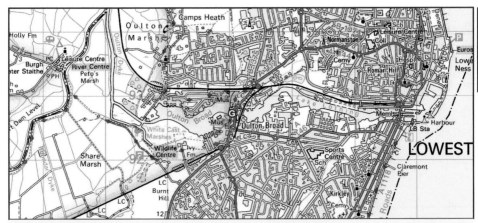

Postcode: NR33 9JS   **Lat N52:28:25**   **Long W01:42:32**

Road Directions

The A146 and A12 both have junctions with the A1117 which are signposted to Oulton Broad, the location. To access Bridge Road from the south, after crossing the railway at Oulton Broad South and passing a church on your right, take the Bridge Road turn just before the roundabout.

From the north go over the bridge, use the rounadabout to make a U turn, get into the left hand lane and turn into Bridge Road. You can park on Bridge Road where there is time limited roadside parking and a car park.

3) Oliver Cromwell heads south towards Beccles and then on to Ipswich with 'The Easterling' Railtour.
Photo by Chris Boon, August, 16:40, 85mm

Worlingham, Marsh Lane Crossing

Location Notes

Situated to the north edge of the village of Worlingham, this road crossing connects the A146 with some moorings on the Broads.

1) Network Rail's unique, end of build, Sprinter 950001 on a test run along the East Suffolk Line heads to Beccles.
   Photo by Steve Goodrum, March, 12:45, 75mm

Public Transport

First Eastern Counties service X2 operates between Lowestoft and Norwich on a roughly half hourly basis. From the Garden Lane bus stop it is a 10 minute walk along Lowestoft Road and then up Marsh Lane to the location.

National Express East Anglia operates services to Beccles Station from Ipswich and Lowestoft.

Amenities

Beccles has a Morrison's store on the A146 with a cafe and petrol station.

Photographic Notes

The primary shot is of Lowestoft bound traffic and should be well lit until around midday. There is a good view of traffic approaching from the Beccles direction as there is a long straight visible between the row of trees. There is no useful shot from the northern side of the line as the view is restricted either by trees or the house opposite the crossing.

2) 37601 and 37087 jet their way towards Lowestoft.
   Photo by Steve Philpott, 11:45, 100mm

There are also trees on the river bank that would spoil a wider, side on, view.

The road is very sparsely used and there are are very few sources of noise to interfere with audio recordings and there is plenty of room for tripods for videographers.

Worlingham, Marsh Lane Crossing

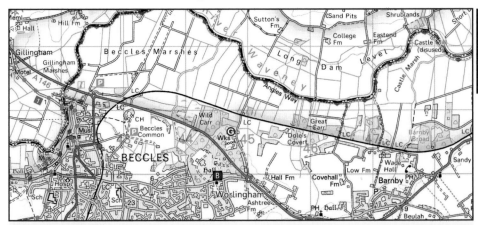

Postcode: NR34 7PF   **Lat N52:27:40**   **Long W01:36:14**

Road Directions

Take either the A12/A145 from the south, the A143 from the west or the A146 from the north and follow the road signs into Beccles. Then follow the signs towards Lowestoft. Once out of Beccles, after crossing the railway, continue down the A146 to the next roundabout. Marsh Lane is signposted from both directions. Turn into Marsh Lane continuing along the no through road, avoiding the right turn onto the old Lowestoft Road and you will reach the location.

There is space for a couple of cars to park but do not block the lane as residents may need access to the other side of the crossing.

3) Heading 'The East Anglian' tour towards Lowestoft, 40145 whistles through the Suffolk countryside.
Photo by Steve Philpott, April, 13:45, 60mm

Beccles Crossing

Location Notes
Situated on the northern edge of the small town of Beccles this is an automatic half barrier crossing on the East Suffolk Line. The location is on the A146 so there will be plenty of traffic passing.

1) 20305 leading 20304 on an Ipswich bound RHTT working, approaches the bend into Beccles on a clockwise circuit.
Photo by Brian Carter, October, 15:45:, 75mm

Public Transport
You can take a train from Ipswich, or Norwich via Lowestoft, to Beccles. Then either follow the footpath across the bridge and turn left across the golf course or leave and turn right up the road until you reach the Morrison's roundabout. Then turn right to reach the crossing. Both routes will be around a 10 minute walk.

Amenities
The Morrison's store opposite the location has a cafe and petrol station.

2) Tailing a clockwise RHTT 37069 passes the crossing.
Photo by Brian Carter, October, 13:45, 75mm

Photographic Notes
For southbound trains the line curves in from the east. There is a large signal cabinet box on the north east corner of the crossing which forces either a tight head on shot or a wide side on view of approaching workings.

Looking south, the line is on a more gentle curve with the Beccles Church dominating the skyline, this is more suited to a telephoto lens style of shot.

The crossing has warbling sirens that would interfere with audio recordings, as would engine noise from any vehicles waiting at the crossing.

3) 170205 approaches Beccles with the Church visible.
August, 07:00, 130mm

Beccles Crossing

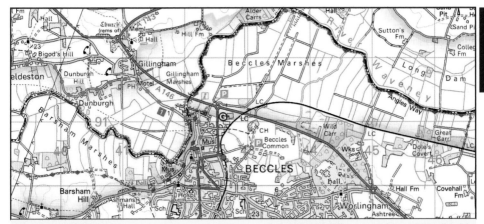

Postcode: NR34 9EJ   **Lat N52:27:50**   **Long W01:34:30**

Road Directions

From the A47 (Norwich by-pass section) take the A146, following the signs for Lowestoft and continue for about 12 miles until you reach the Beccles Roundabout. Continue across the roundabout, past Morrison's on the right and you will reach the crossing a few hundred yards down the road. From the south, take the A12, leaving on the A145 after Blythbiurgh. Continue to Beccles, about 12 miles and drive through the town on the A145. Turn right onto the A146 at the roundabout. There are lay-bys on either side of the crossing, but failing that, you could use the Morrison's car park.

4) Warbling their way towards Beccles 20305 tops up with 20304 on the clockwise East Suffolk Line circuit.
Photo by Brian Carter, October, 13:45, 75mm

Weston Crossings

Location Notes
On the East Suffolk line roughly midway between Beccles and Halesworth, the locations are three crossings between fields.

1) 33103 pushes *Caroline* to crossing #1. The embankments have grown since, but this view shows the gradient north.
April, 13:45, 80mm

Public Transport
Anglian Bus & Coach, service 521, operates almost hourly between Beccles Old Market, which is straight down Station Road and then right on 'The Walk', to Ringsfield. From where it would be a 15 minute walk.

Amenities
There is nothing around the location, the nearest would be in Ringsfield village where there is the Horseshoes Pub that serves food and drink 7 days a week.

Photographic Notes
There are 3 distinct crossings here. The northern two (#2 and #3) are foot crossings and the southern is one (#1) is an automatic half barrier road crossing with the location in a field entrance.

2) 170206 up the bank towards Beccles. #2
February, 12:15, 105mm

The line runs slightly north east at the location, so crossing #3 should be good for shots until late morning as it has no view from the west of the line. The other two can be shot from both sides in both directions, so they can be used at any time during daylight hours. Southbound is downhill so workings will not be powering much. The top of the climb is opposite crossing #3. Trees are beginning to grow at the location which, without attention, will begin to encroach on shots. You might like a step ladder to get over them. Crossing #3 is bordered by fences with stiles so you can get a height boost from them.

3) 170206 heads to Lowestoft passing crossing#3.
July, 08:00, 35mm

Weston Crossings

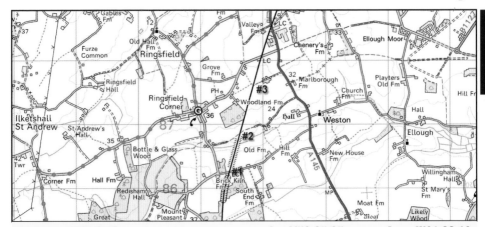

Postcode: NR34 8NT   **Lat N52:25:35**   **Long W01:33:10**

Road Directions

From Beccles take the A145 south. After crossing the railway continue down the road taking the fourth right turn into Kings Lane. From the south, take the A12, leaving on the A145 after Blythbiurgh. Continue towards Beccles and after passing through Willingham and Willingham St Mary, take the second turning left into Kings Lane. Follow this road and you will reach crossing number #1. There is a lay-by next to the crossing but other than that the lane is quite narrow, so park carefully off the road. For the other two crossings you will need to park off the A145, or in Ringsfield Village and walk to the crossings.

4) Behind ever growing veg, 70013 heads 'The Easterling' south towards Ipswich on the approaches to crossing #1
Photo by Steve Goodrum, May, 09:00, 75mm

North Norfolk - 'Bittern Line'

General Notes

Taking it's name from one of Norfolk's indigenous wild birds, the 'Bittern Line' extends around 30 miles from the city of Norwich to Sheringham on the North Norfolk coast.

A large section of the line, from North Walsham to Sheringham, is single track with passing loops. The line requires a reversal at Cromer to reach Sheringham, so all workings up the line will either be units or Top and Tailed locomotives.

Unlike the East Suffolk Line, which uses RETB signalling, the Bittern Line is all Track Circuit Block from Norwich to Cromer. Then Tokenless block working on the short section from Cromer to Sheringham.

1) 156409 east to Cromer through Beeston Regis.
Photo by Albert Dawson, September, 12:15, 55mm

Passenger Traffic

The line is usually worked by a pair of units from the Norwich Crown Point fleet. These include 153s, 156s and 170s. The decision is solely in the hands of the local operator, National Express East Anglia but this franchise will expire in March 2011.

Freight Traffic

Currently there is an as-required weekday service conveying gas condensate waste from the North Walsham terminal to the Essex port of Harwich.

The trains, run on behalf of Carless Petrochemicals and are usually formed of a GBRf Class 66 loco and 18 100-tonne TEA bogie tankers.

2) 37069 and 059 head a RHTT towards Norwich.
Photo by Steve Goodrum, October, 15:45, 180mm

Occasional Traffic

Until 2010, charter traffic was sparse and very irregular. However, with the opening of the link between the National Network and the North Norfolk Railway, charters will become more commonplace as will locomotive moves to the railway.

In the autumn the line is covered by the Stowmarket based RHTT operations, which have recently been operated by Direct Rail Services class 37s. With 20s, 57s and even 66s appearing from time to time.

Serco test trains are very rare on this section of the line, with perhaps 2 or 3 visits a year.

3) Operating a shuttle service, the B1 at Wroxham.
Photo by Ian Bowskill, September, 12:15, 55mm

North Norfolk - 'Bittern Line'

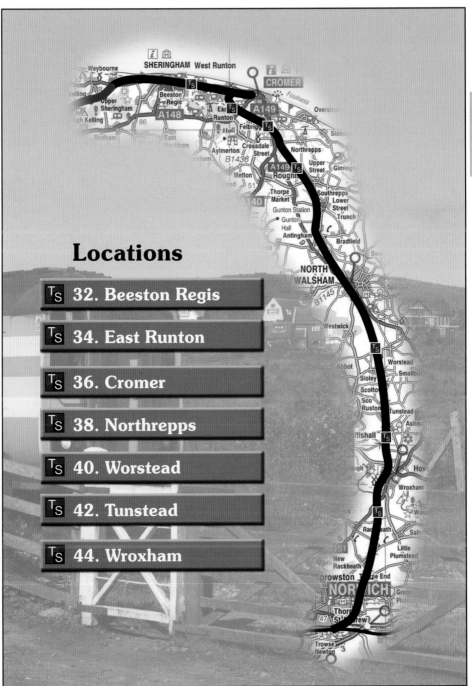

Locations

T_S	32. Beeston Regis
T_S	34. East Runton
T_S	36. Cromer
T_S	38. Northrepps
T_S	40. Worstead
T_S	42. Tunstead
T_S	44. Wroxham

Beeston Regis

Location Notes
This location is in open, school playing fields in the village of Beeston Regis, just south of the coast. To the north of the line are caravan parks and a small church. The sea breeze can make it quite windy.

1) Slightly outside the usual haunts for 'Hastings' units, 1001 heads west along the coast towards Sheringham.
   Photo by Calum Hepplewhite, November, 12:10, 65mm

Public Transport
Saunders, Norfolk Green and First Eastern Counties all operate services from Sheringham to Beeston Regis. You will need the Beeston Hall stop just after Beeston Regis Village.

Amenities
There is a 'Spar' store and a petrol station in West Runton, about a 5-10 minute walk from the location.

Accommodation
There is plenty of seasonal holiday accommodation in the area.

Photographic Notes
There is scope for both wide and tight shots from the south of the line but due to the trees and chalets in the area there is no wide angle from the north of the line. There is only a tight but pleasant curve shot for a morning eastbound working. Speed restriction signs at the crossing mean westbound shots are not possible but you can walk to the other side of the field.

2) The west bound shot from the coast side, on the curve.
   January, 12:10, 50mm

The openness of the location and it's proximity to the coast mean the location can get quite windy, making audio recordings difficult.

Beeston Regis

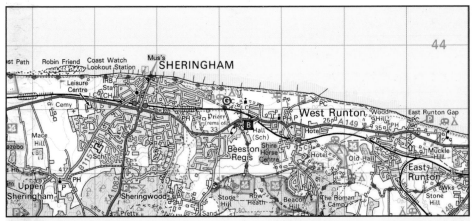

Postcode: NR27 9QZ **Lat N52:56:24** **Long E01:13:46**

Road Directions

The location is on the A149 between Sheringham and Cromer. The turning for the railway line is opposite the Beeston Hall Co-Ed Prep school. It leads to their playing fields and also to the caravan park and church on the coastal side of the railway.

The playing fields have an area for parking a few cars on the eastern side which is off the road to the crossing as opposed to the road under the railway line bridge.

3) More usual traction for the route in the shape of 156418 heading east towards Cromer, then reversal to Norwich.
Photo by Calum Hepplewhite, November, 11:45, 40mm

East Runton

Location Notes
The locations are the site of the former junction where the line split to go to Sheringham or Cromer before the western curve of the triangle was lifted over 50 years ago. Trains, therefore, have to reverse at Cromer station. The two locations here favour different directions.

1) From the Holt Road lay-by, a 156 cuts through the Norfolk countryside on the way to Cromer.
January , 09:15, 110mm

Public Transport
National Express East Anglia operates a service to Cromer Station from Norwich. From there it is about a mile along Holt Road to the location.

Amenities
Holt Road has a petrol station very close to the location. Further down the road are a number of shops including a Morrison's Store, with a cafe, opposite Cromer Station.
In the town are various chip shops and fast food outlets.

Accommodation
Cromer is a holiday town, so has a number of guest houses and hotels. There are also many caravan parks in the area.

Photographic Notes
For northbound trains to Cromer, the Holt Road bridge offers a sweeping shot of the line curving round, or from the lay-by you can get a wide, scenic shot, across the fields. For trains heading to Norwich you can move round to the fields in Green Lane and get the train on the embankment.

East Runton

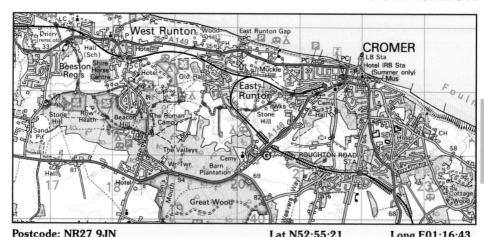

Postcode: NR27 9JN   **Lat N52:55:21**   **Long E01:16:43**

Road Directions

Take either the A140, from the south, or the A149, from the south east into Cromer and then follow the signs for Kings Lynn and Fakenham out on the A148.

Or if driving from Kings Lynn follow the A148 towards Cromer.

On the outskirts of Cromer, before the railway if exiting the town, there is a large lay-by opposite the police station where you can park.

For the southbound shot, continue up Holt Road out of Cromer and take the left into Greens Lane which you can follow downhill to the other location. Given the narrow nature of this lane it may be worth driving between the two locations. There are a few field entrances to park in on Greens Lane.

2) Used to a diet of Sprinter units, the sheep run for cover as the B1 heads south with the Cromer Dido special shuttle.
Photo by Ian Bowskill, April, 14:30, 90mm

Cromer, A149 Bridge

Location Notes

This location is on the southern edge of Cromer, about ¼ of a mile east of Rougton Road Station. As this is on the main road from Norwich there will be plenty of traffic passing by.

1) 156418 heads south towards North Walsham with a local service bound for Norwich
January, 10:00, 95mm

Public Transport

Saunders coaches, services 44/45, operate between Norwich and Sheringham and will call at the The Avenue stop in Cromer which is just past the location.

Amenities

There is nothing in the immediate area but Cromer has a wide range of shops.

Accommodation

Cromer has a range of Bed and Breakfasts, hotels and caravan parks.

Photographic Notes

The line runs north east to south west at this point so southbound shots will be on until mid-afternoon. The line is in a cutting but the sides are set back a reasonable distance and should not pose a shadow problem during the middle of the day.

The bridge has low sided parapets which are easy to see over but the southbound pavement is quite narrow, approximately 2 feet, so it would not be the best place to stand for a long time next to the busy road. The road noise causes problems for audio recordings.

Cromer, A149 Bridge

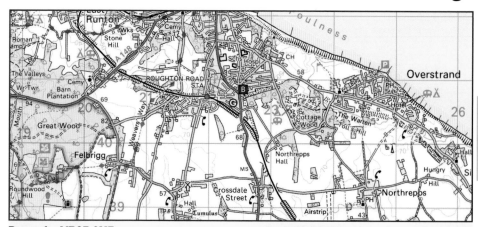

Postcode: NR27 0HZ   **Lat N52:54:54**   **Long E01:18:29**

Road Directions

The A149 joins the A140 about ¾ of a mile south of the location so follow either of these from the south towards Cromer. From the north or east take the A148 to Cromer and then the A149 south. The bridge is on the southern outskirts of the town and is just after the 40mph speed limit begins. There is a set of power lines crossing the road as an extra visual reference.

There are a few residential streets close by where you can park and the turning into The Avenue is wide enough for a couple of cars.

2) B1 61264 and the short charter set head south during the days special 'Cromer Dido' shuttles.
Photo by Ian Bowskill, April, 11:30, 70mm

Northrepps

Location Notes

A few miles to the south of Cromer, this is a road bridge in rural Norfolk farm land.

1) 156422 ignores the snowflakes on the way north towards Sheringham and Cromer.
January, 10:20, 50mm

Public Transport

Saunders Coaches, services 33/4/5, operate between North Walsham and Cromer. These stop in Thorpe Market village from where it will be about a 15 minute walk to the location.

Amenities

There is nothing in the immediate area. There are some local shops in Thorpe Market and larger stores in Cromer to the north.

Accommodation

Green Hill Farm hotel in Thorpe Market has a restaurant and accommodation.

Photographic Notes

The line is very straight approaching from the north and the embankments up to the bridge will require long lenses to get past the bank shadows. The line is also on a climb heading south so southbound workings should be under power.

Heading north the line curves into the cutting and will be backlit and in shadow for much of the day.

The bridge has reasonably high parapets and a step ladder would be an advantage to get over these.

Also, the area is open to the elements and audio may suffer from wind noise.

Northrepps

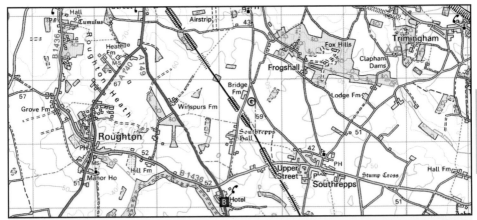

Postcode: NR27 0LQ   **Lat N52:53:16**   **Long E01:19:58**

Road Directions

Leave the A149 at the crossroads just to the north of Thorpe Market and take the easterly exit onto Thorpe Road - right if coming out of the village, left if coming from the north. A very short distance up the road take the left fork and continue, passing The Southern Rhodesia Memorial Avenue on your right, to the bridge. There is a large farm yard to the north of the bridge where you can turn your vehicle.

2) DRS 37s 069 and 059 head a rail head treatment train south towards Norwich.
Photo by Steve Goodrum, October, 15:45, 180mm

Worstead, Obelisk Lane

Location Notes

This is an over bridge on a bridleway to Worstead Village about ¾ of a mile from Worstead Station and 10 miles from Norwich. There is a field where lorry trailers are stored and a private residence next to the path. There is also the private estate of Westwick House to the west.

1) With St Marys Church providing the backdrop, 156418 scuttles north towards the coast at Cromer.
January, 11:00, 95mm

Public Transport

The location is a 10 to 15 minute walk from Worstead railway station, which is served by National Express Anglia services from Norwich and Sheringham.

Amenities

There is nothing in the immediate area. The nearest town with any range of facilities is Wroxham, about 4 or 5 miles to the south by road, which has plenty of cafes, shops and food outlets.

Accommodation

Wroxham has a number of guest houses and hotels.

Photographic Notes

The bridge is contained in a spinney of trees which throw long shadows for most of the day so longer lenses will be preferable at this location to get past the shadows. The line is also climbing towards North Walsham so most southbound workings will be coasting at this point.

Being in open countryside there are few sources of noise, other than the wind, to interfere with audio recordings.

2) 66725 heads south with the 'Walsham Tanks'.
Photo by Jonathan Cordle, May, 14:300, 300mm

Worstead, Obelisk Lane

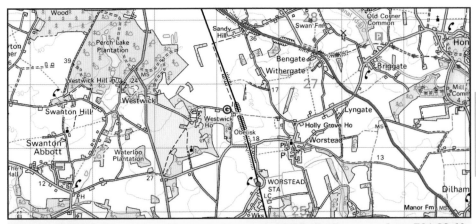

Postcode: NR28 0JD **Lat N52:47:15** **Long E01:23:60**

Road Directions

From the A140 north of Norwich, follow the signs to Coltishall on the A1354 and then, in Coltishall, take the B1150 north towards North Walsham. After passing Coltishall airfield and Scottow hamlet turn right at the crossroads following the signs to Worstead Station and the brown "Abbey" tourist symbol for about ½ a mile. You will see the railway in front of you. Before the railway is a left hand turn, this is Obelisk Lane. There are a few places along the road up to the location where you could park a car, but be careful. The road, although sparsely used, can be used for large farm machinery and lorries so leave plenty of space.

3) Split box thrash from 37087 as it tackles the climb towards North Walsham with an RHTT working.
Photo by Steve Jonathan Cordle, November, 12:00, 80mm

Tunstead, Belaugh Lane

Location Notes

This is a road with a small manually operated gate crossing situated in open farmland, with the village of Tunstead about half a mile to the north and the village of Coltishall about a mile west along the road.

1) DRS Bodysnatchers 57011 and 57009 cross Belaugh Lane with a RHTT working towards Sheringham.
Photo by Steve Goodrum, October, 14:30, 75mm

Public Transport

The location is linked to the village of Wroxham by the only privately-owned footpath in Norfolk and is a short 1½ mile walk.

Amenities

The Wroxham Barns has toilets and a cafe that are open every day from 10:00 to 17:00.

Accommodation

Wroxham has a number of guest houses and hotels.

Photographic Notes

The location offers a south bound shot from the eastern side of the line, or a north bound shot from the western side of the line. There is, currently, a large mound of earth surrounding the parking that you can use to gain height for southbound workings. Aside from a few trees there is nothing to cast shadows in the area but a step ladder may be useful to get above some of the line side vegetation in the area.

2) 156422 ambles north towards North Walsham.
January, 12:00, 70mm

Tunstead, Belaugh Lane

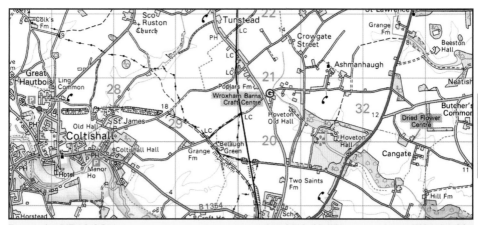

Postcode: NR12 8QU   **Lat N52:43:57**   **Long W01:24:22**

Road Directions

From Norwich take the A1151 north east to Wroxam, passing through the village centre. Cross over the river and follow the signs for Wroxham Barns and, after passing the barns, take the next left at the crossroad with the Tunstead Village Sign (A model of a man with a barrel in a shed) on to Belaugh Lane. Drive down the road to reach the location.

There is a large area, opposite the crossing, in the corner of the field to park in.

3) 61264 on one of the day's many Dido shuttles, heads north toward Sheringham with 33025 on the rear.
Photo by Steve Goodrum, April, 17:45, 75mm

Wroxham, Bear's Grove Crossing

Location Notes

Just to the south of Wroxham, this is a foot crossing on a farm track about 3 miles outside Norwich. You are in a countryside area bounded by woods on the west and fields on the east. There is no lighting at the crossing and it would be very muddy after rain.

1) 156418 heads south towards journey's end at Norwich with one of the shuttle services from Sheringham.
   January, 12:30, 95mm

Public Transport

Anglian Bus and Coach operates a number of services from Norwich Railway Station to Salhouse and then on to Wroxham. You will need the 'Vicarage Road, Bell Lane' stop. From there it is a 5 minute walk to the location.

Amenities

There is nothing at the location, but Wroxham has a wide range of shops and cafes. Failing that, Norwich is a few miles to the south.

Photographic Notes

The line is quite straight and runs north to south through the location. Shadows from the trees will cause problems in the afternoon when the sun has come round to the western side of the line but a step ladder on the edge of the field will get round this.

There is only the sound of the roads in the distance to interfere with audio recordings.

2) 156422 heading south seen from the crossing gates .
   Photo by Ian Bowskill, April, 09:30, 55mm

Wroxham, Bear's Grove Crossing

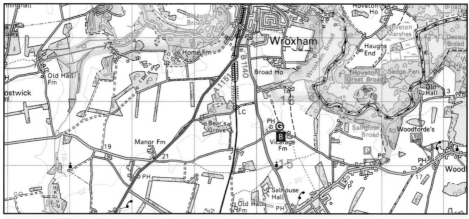

Postcode: NR13 6HD　　　　　　　**Lat N52:41:30**　　　　　　　**Long E01:23:49**

Road Directions

Take the A1151 out of Norwich towards Wroxham. About ½ a mile before Wroxham is a lay-by on the left just before the Bear's Grove private road turning. You can park here easily and walk down the lane to the crossing.

Alternatively, continue into Wroxham. After crossing the railway turn right and follow the road round. Shortly after passing a spur off the road on the left there is a dip in the road and then a field entrance on the right. This is the other end of Bear's Grove. Park carefully here as the lane is unsuitable for road traffic and there is nowhere to turn round at the end.

3) B1 61264 is towed north by 33025 past the crossing on the 'Dido' shuttle service to Sheringham.
Photo by Ian Bowskill, April, 10:00, 55mm

Ipswich to Sizewell and Felixstowe

General Notes

The line from Sizewell to Westerfield, is signalled by the Radio Electronic Token Block (RETB) and any unit, or locomotive, needs to be suitably equipped for this. See the East Suffolk line chapter for details. The Felixstowe branch is conventionally signalled, with the entire branch being single track after the Westerfield junction.

The branch is earmarked for a number of major expansion projects over the next few years including re-doubling of the line between Trimley and Westerfield Junction.

A new freight only east to north curve bypassing East Suffolk Junction is to be added. The 'Bacon curve' will mean that Cross Country intermodal traffic will not need to reverse in Ipswich Yards, as is currently the case. It will also mean that some traffic to the Midlands, that was routed via London, can use the Bury St Edmumds line when that line is upgraded to W10 Gauge standards to accommodate 9ft 6in containers.

These projects, combined with the internal expansion of the port itself, creating a third rail head to the north west of the current northern terminal, will see traffic on the line continue to increase.

Passenger Traffic

The Felixstowe branch is operated by a single unit, either a 153 or 156, shuttling to Ipswich. The East Suffolk line is worked by the Norwich Crown Point fleet of RETB units. These include 153s, 156s and 170s.

Freight Traffic

There is only one 'regular' working to Sizewell. Locally know as the 'Sizewell Coal' this is a DRS operated service. This service runs on an as required basis back to Sellafield in Cumbria. Felixstowe is the UK's largest container port and as such the line has more freight traffic than passenger. With traffic from all the larger operators there is a constant stream of intermodal traffic to both the north and south dock terminals.

Occasional Traffic

Neither line is well frequented by charter traffic and test trains usually operate during the night, owing to the frequency of daytime trains. The East Suffolk line sees RHTT traffic in the autumn, but the Felixstowe Branch's volume of traffic means the leaves do not get a chance to settle.

1) 153309 shuttles up & down the Felixstowe Branch.
Juky 09:45, 45mm

2) 66538 speeds east with an intermodal.
July, 14:45, 45mm

3) Route learning 'Ped' style on the Sizewell branch.
Photo by Nigel Hutcihson, March, 15:45, 55mm

Ipswich to Sizewell and Felixstowe

Locations

- T S 48. Felixstowe Nth Docks
- T S 50. Clickett Hill
- T S 52. Grimstone Lane
- T S 54. Morston Hall
- T S 56. Levington
- T S 58. Tuddenham Road
- T S 60. Leiston
- T S 62. Martlesham
- T S 64. Little Bealings
- T S 66. Westerfield
- T S 68. East Suffolk Junc

Felixstowe North Docks

Location Notes
These locations are on public footpaths bordering the docks northern terminal.

Public Transport
First Eastern Counties, service 75, runs from Ipswich Cattle Market to the Morrision's Store on Grange Farm. From there you need to walk down Hintlesham Drive and then onto Rendlesham Road. Take the footpath on the other side of the houses across the footbridge into the field. Continue down the path and then follow the road south. Currently this road is closed to vehicular traffic, but when the port expands it will be used.

At the roundabout follow the road to the right, Blofield Road, and then left onto Parker Avenue. At the end of Parker Avenue you will see the terminal to your right, walk along the road for views. Walking time will be around 20-30 minutes

1) 70001 shunts around the terminal's west end.
December, 13:30, 50mm

Amenities
There are plenty of fish and chip shops on the sea front and a McDonald's drive through is located off the A14, first roundabout, into Felixstowe.

Accommodation
Felixstowe is a holiday town and there are numerous hotels and guest houses in the town.

Photographic Notes
There are two public vantage points here around the dock terminal.

First, from the road side. There is a high chain mesh fence here. Wide shots from across the road or a step ladder, will avoid this.

2) 66569 stands by the gates awaiting departure.
Photo by Michael Proudfoot, May, 16:30, 40mm

Second, from the footpaths. From the western end of the terminal there is a footpath across the terminal lines. The footpath is, obviously, closed during shunting movements but you can get shots from the gate sides. There are also angles on the trains being loaded inside the terminal. If you follow the path round to the right from the entrance you can also get through a number of gaps in the bramble hedge to get views of the curve out of the docks. This, however, would be quite tricky during wet weather. The gradient is quite steep coming out of the docks so a loaded liner will be working quite hard to get the train moving and climb the grade up towards Trimley.

3) From the bank top a wide view of the terminal.
March, 14:15, 75mm

Felixstowe North Docks

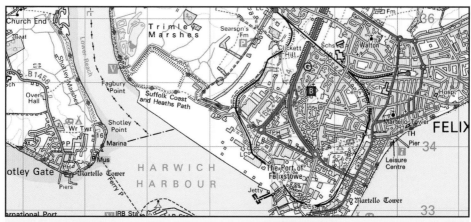

Postcode: IP11 2YP   **Lat N51:57:47**   **Long E01:18:32**

Road Directions

Take the A14 into Felixstowe and after passing under the railway and the white girder bridge take the exit left and then turn left into the housing area. Morrison's Supermarket will be ahead of you but you should turn left up the hill on Grange Farm Avenue. Take the next left onto Hintlesham Drive and follow this road round to Rendlesham Road.

Park, considerately, on Rendlesham Road and follow the foot directions in the public transport notes.

4) 66715 soaks up the seaside sun while awaiting its next duty. Taken on steps by the fence line, foot crossing behind.
August, 10:30, 35mm

Felixstowe, Clickett Hill

Location Notes

This location consists of a foot crossing and embankment locations in open farmland between the industrial areas bordering the port of Felixstowe and the village of Trimley. The public footpath runs through private land on the Trimley side. There are woods for shelter but that aside, the area is quite open to the elements.

1) Pioneer 'PowerHaul' 70001 lifts the first daylight working for the class out from the docks heading for Lawley Street.
Photo by Geoff Tibble, December, 14:15, 80mm

Public Transport

Trimley Station is served by an hourly Ipswich to Felixstowe Town service. First Eastern Counties operates a number of buses from Ipswich 'Old Cattle Market' to Trimley which takes about an hour.

Amenities

There are a few shops in Trimley.

Photographic Notes

The shot from above the embankment favours dock departures until around 11:00 after which the sun will come off the front. After lunch anything arriving will be well lit.

2) 57001 descends with an intermodal from Daventry.
Photo by Michael Proudfoot, May, 15:00, 50mm

The crossing is a fairly head-on shot with the line running pretty much north to south. The line up to the crossing is bordered by trees which will cast shadows over trains exiting the docks when the sun is low.

The line has a steep gradient coming out of the docks towards Trimley and given the curvature of the line it is possible to get an *'American' style* shot of the front of the train with the back of the train snaking away behind it.

For video the trains will coast down the bank, so will only really make flange squealing noises but that aside, you have the distant noise of the docks to add to the ambience.

3) 66569 with a light loco move into the North Dock.
Photo by Michael Proudfoot, May, 16:00, 35mm

Felixstowe, Clickett Hill

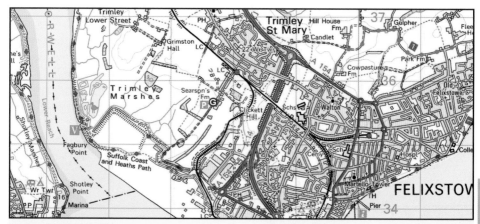

Postcode: IP11 0UD   **Lat N51:58:15**   **Long E01:19:12**

Road Directions

From the A14 heading towards Felixstowe: Leave at the Trimley exit (Junction 60, signposted Trimley / Kirton). At the roundabout turn left along High Road and the station, on Station Road, is signposted. There are two options for parking. The station car park is before the level crossing and there is a parking area at the end of the Cordys Lane.

Then, on foot, take the 'Blofield Track' bridleway off Cordys Lane. Do not be tempted to follow the footpath closer to the station as this runs through private farm land and is a very difficult walk. Walk down the bridleway and you will reach the railway which is on a bridge/embankment above you. Either turn left and walk down the footpath, which leads to the docks, for another few hundred yards to reach the foot crossing; or go under the bridge and turn right then climb the embankment for the raised shots.

4) 66572 crawls down the bank with an intermodal.
Photo by Oli Smith, June, 13:30, 120mm

Trimley St Martin, Grimstone Lane

Location Notes

This location is on a quiet road surrounded by fields and a few houses. There is no livestock in the vicinity as the farming in the area is predominately arable.

1) 70001 heads towards Felixstowe with an intermodal, taken from opposite the north western level crossing.
   Photo by Geoff Tibble, December, 13:15, 35mm

Public Transport

There is a regular, hourly, train service from Ipswich to Trimley. Leave Trimley station car park and turn right, walking down the road until you reach a T-Junction. From here, turn left and walk down the High Road all the way out of Trimley until you reach Grimstone Lane on the left. Walking time about 30 minutes. Bus numbers are 75, 75A, 76 and 77, these services are regular on weekdays and the stop is opposite Grimstone Lane and they also stop near the rail station. The location is a short walk from the main road.

Amenities

A local post office and village store are situated between this location and Trimley station on High Road. Plus the The Hand in Hand pub. There is also Gullivers chip shop on Kingsbury Road in Trimley village.

Photographic Notes

Shots here are primarily of Felixstowe bound workings, from either the level or foot crossing locations. Due to trees there is no Ipswich bound shot from the level crossing, only from the foot crossing.

The time between crossing barriers lowering and the train passing is quite short, but this is not a problem for trains heading towards Ipswich as there are several whistle boards before this location so trains are audible before becoming visible.

The foot crossing has the former keeper's house as the backdrop.

2) 66715 heads west towards the foot crossing.
   Photo by James Welham, May, 12:15, 450mm

Trimley St Martin, Grimstone Lane

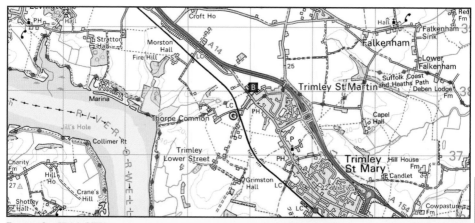

Postcode: IP11 0RX   **Lat N51:59:24**   **Long E01:18:10**

Road Directions

From the A14, leave at junction 59, then at the roundabout take the 3rd exit (signposted Trimley Villages) Enter Trimley, then at the 2nd roundabout, take the 3rd exit onto High Road (entering Trimley St. Martin). Take the first left turn into Grimstone Lane and continue to the location. There is space for one car to park just over the level crossing, and a further space 50 yards or so if you turn left immediately after going over the crossing.

It is very safe to leave your car, the majority of traffic on the quiet lane is farm machinery.

3) 70001 heads, past the foot crossing, towards Felixstowe with a loaded intermodal from Lawley Street.
Photo by Calum Hepplewhite, December, 13:30, 45mm

Trimley St Martin, Morston Hall

Location Notes

This location is in the open farmland to the north of Trimley, the northern location is roadside and the southern is a footpath.

1) The unusual sight of DRS hire-in 66419 speeding westwards with a Freightliner intermodal towards Ipswich.
Photo by David Smith, March, 16:!5, 115mm

Public Transport

Trains from Ipswich to Trimley are hourly. Leave the station and head into the village. At the T-junction turn left and walk out of the village. Continue until you reach Goslings farm shop on your left and take the Morston Hall Road turning on the left. You will see the railway line on your left. The next left turning, also Morston Hall Road, will lead you up to the crossing and the location.

The number 75/76 buses run from Ipswich to Trimley. You could get off either at Strattonhall Drift, opposite the boat shop or at the first stop in Trimley Village as both are an equal distance to the location.

Amenities

The Orwell Crossing lorry park, to the west on the A14, is open 24 hours with restaurant and washroom facilities. There are also a few local shops in Trimley.

Accommodation

None in the immediate area, but there is plenty in Felixstowe.

2) 66591 heads a Felixstowe to Tilbury intermodal.
Photo by James Welham, May, 08:10, 200mm

Photographic Notes

The line is fairly straight and on a slight embankment and with no trees on the lineside there is little to cast shadows on your subject. The lighting will work best for Felixstowe bound workings until just after lunchtime, then it will favour Ipswich bound workings. Given the open nature of the location there will be plenty of notice of approaching trains in the distance.

The crossing barriers are of the automatic half barrier type and as such will always be 'warbling' when there is a train passing, which might put some videographers off.

Trimley St Martin, Morston Hall

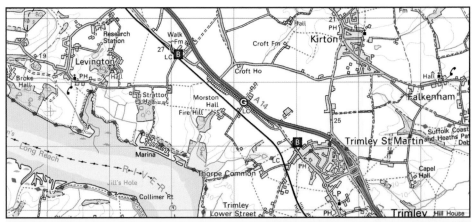

Postcode: IP11 0SQ   **Lat N51:59:56**   **Long E01:17:32**

Road Directions

From the A14 leave at junction 59, then at the roundabout take the 3rd exit (signposted Trimley Villages)
Enter Trimley then at 2nd roundabout, take the 3rd exit onto 'High Road' (Entering Trimley St.Martin).
Continue along the High Road all the way out of Trimley and turn left after the Garden Centre, do not rejoin
the A14. Morston Hall is signposted off the road and is the next left turning.
Park off road before the railway and make sure you leave enough room for vehicles to get past.
Do not park on the other side of the crossing.

3) With the level crossing in the background, 66580 powers an intermodal towards Felixstowe docks.
Photo by David Smith, December, 13:45, 100mm

Levington

Location Notes

The location is a road over bridge. There is little near the location other than fields and a 'research station' a short distance down the road.

1) From a foot crossing west of the main bridge, 66580 heads to Ipswich with an intermodal to Hams Hall.
   Photo by John Tomlinson, April, 17:00, 105mm

Public Transport

The First no 77, from Ipswich Cattle Market, passes the bus stops at the end of the road to this location. You can see the location from the bus stop.

Amenities

The Orwell Crossing lorry park, to the west on the A14, is open 24 hours with restaurant and washroom facilities.

Accommodation

There is none in the immediate vicinity but there is plenty of holiday type accommodation in Felixstowe.

Photographic Notes

The line under the bridge runs south east at this point and as such is well lit for all the morning and a good part of the early afternoon. After that the foot crossing to the west is better lit.

2) 70001 speeds towards the docks with an intermodal.
   July, 10:15, 200mm

Dock bound trains can be seen approaching from about a mile away, they appear from behind a big oval shaped tree and continue round a sweeping curve to the long straight to the bridge.

The bridge parapets are quite high and a step ladder would be required to see over them. Fortunately the bridge edges are waist height 'armco' and can easily be seen over.

Levington

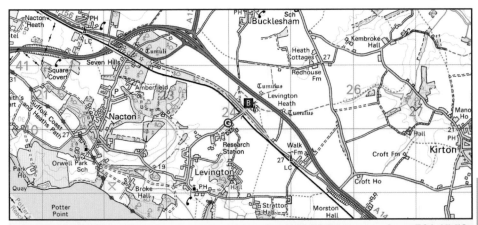

Postcode: IP10 0JE   **Lat N52:00:54**   **Long E01:15:58**

Road Directions

After crossing the Orwell Bridge continue along the A14 for about 3 miles, pass one junction (Junction 57), go under the railway and then under a road bridge and leave the A14 at Junction 58. Take the third exit towards Nacton and drive for about 400 yards until the road bends to the right. There is a turning on the left (Felixstowe Road) take it and follow this road to the location. When the road becomes a short dual carriageway look out for the bridge on your right and take the, aptly named, Bridge Road to the location. On the northern side of the bridge is a very wide strip of grass that will accommodate a number of cars.

3) Freightliner's 66578 powers a morning Intermodal from Tilbury, seen from the northen side of the bridge.
July, 10:15, 40mm

Ipswich, Tuddenham Road

Location Notes

The location is a road over bridge over a cutting on the outskirts of Ipswich with open fields to the north. The road is quite busy and the edges are quite narrow so be careful.

1) 37069 & 20304 slow on the approach to Westerfield for RETB token collection on an Ipswich to Lowestoft RHTT.
Photo by Tom Jenkins, December, 13:00, 300mm

Public Transport

Far East Travel operates the number 70 service from Ipswich Cattle Market to the Millennium Cemetery. From here it is a short walk along the Tuddenham Road to the bridge.

Amenities

There is nothing at the location, you will have to go further into Ipswich.

Photographic Notes

The bridge parapets are quite high and a step ladder will be required to see over them on anything other than tip toes. There is no pavement to speak of, just a kerb area about a foot wide.

Anything heading north will be climbing away after stopping for the RETB token exchange at Westerfield.

Due to the width of the kerb this location would be unsuitable for video work as there is insufficient space to set up a tripod safely.

2) 37087 leads 37261 as they head north up the line.
Photo by Peter Foster, October, 09:15, 85mm

Ipswich, Tuddenham Road

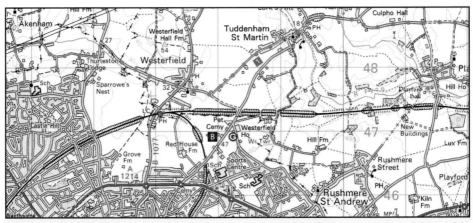

Postcode: IP4 3QG   **Lat N52:04:51**   **Long E01:11:06**

Road Directions

From the north, exit the A14 at Junction 53, or from the south at Junction 55 and follow the road into Ipswich until you reach the junction with the A1214. Take the ring road anti-clockwise. Follow the signs for the Millennium Cemetery, which is located on Tuddenham Road. Pass the Cemetery on your left and the location is the next bridge a few hundred yards on.

There are a few off-road spots on Church Lane, which is the left turn just after the bridge.

3) After picking up the RETB token from Westerfield 40145 powers up the climb towards Woodbridge and Lowestoft.
Photo by Calum Hepplewhite, April, 12:00, 95mm

Leiston, Farm Crossings

Location Notes
This location is set in farm land in rural Suffolk. As it is fields, expect to get muddy feet after it has been raining. If there are crops in the fields be respectful and only use the field edges.

1) The main destination reached, the 20/20 Vision tour heads back along the branch towards Ipswich.
Photo by James Welham, March, 14:15, 135mm

Public Transport
First Eastern Counties, service 64, operates between Ipswich Cattle Market, Woodbridge and Saxmundham to Leiston. The Clay Hills stop is the closest to the line, just before Leiston Village. Alternatively Saxmundham station is served by trains from Ipswich and Lowestoft and it is about 30 minutes walk to the locations.

Amenities
There are a number of shops in the centre of the Leiston along High Street and Sizewell Road.

2) The NR Sprinter also, occasionally, visits the line.
Photo by Steve Goodrum, March, 10:45, 120mm

Photographic Notes
The line runs roughly east to west so with most of the shots from the southern side of the line, the light will favour morning eastbound and afternoon westbound workings. Trees and lineside vegetation provide an occasional challenge.

As the crossings on the line are manually operated it is very easy to get ahead of workings between crossings as they stop before and after, to let the guard out to open and close the crossings.

Leiston, Farm Crossings

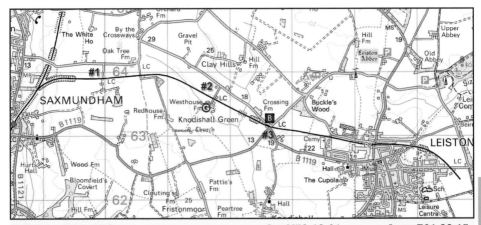

Postcode: IP16 4WG   **Lat N52:13:01**   **Long E01:32:15**

Road Directions

Leave the A12 at the B1121 near Saxmundham, from either the north or south and follow this road towards Saxmundham Village. To the north of the village is a turning to Clay Hills, take this. Crossing #1 is the first right off this road. Continue to the end of the road, turn left and then take the next right. The second house on your right has a road just after it that leads to crossing #2. Crossing #3 is at the end of the road. Once there park, considerately, at the roadside.

3) Pausing for the crossing master to get back in after closing the gates, 37423 and 611 head towards Saxmundham.
Photo by Oli Smith, August, 16:00, dslr@44mm

Martlesham, A12 Bridge

Location Notes
A road bridge on the A12 trunk road between Ipswich and Lowestoft just on the edge of Woodbridge.

1) With a London to Lowestoft working, 170206 ambles east through the Suffolk countryside towards Woodbridge.
February, 11:30, 85mm

Public Transport
The Martlesham Park and Ride terminus is just to the south of the location.
The site is open from 07:00 until 19:00 Mondays to Saturdays. There are 550 parking spaces and parking is free (when using the £2.90 Park & Ride service).
Dedicated Park & Ride buses run to Ipswich town centre every 12 minutes.
From here you will need to walk back up the A12 to reach the location.

Amenities
There is a BP Petrol Station, KFC restaurant and Tesco Extra store on the A12 all a short distance to the south of the location. Woodbridge also has a wide range of shops in the town centre.

Accommodation
There is nothing in the immediate area but there are a number of 'travel inn' type hotels in the Ipswich as well as Bed and Breakfasts in the town of Woodbridge.

Photographic Notes
The line runs east to west so should be well illuminated all day. The bridge sides are quite high so a step ladder may be useful. Because of this it is not possible to see, or hear, what is coming in the opposite direction, so workings may sneak up on you.
Given that the location is a road bridge on the busy A12, audio will be dominated by the sound of passing traffic. It is also not possible to cross the road safely to get 'going away' shots of the working.

Martlesham, A12 Bridge

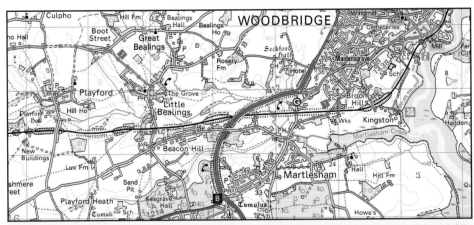

Postcode: IP12 4RA   **Lat N52:04:42**   **Long E01:16:25**

Road Directions

Take the A12 north, past Ipswich, towards Woodbridge. Or take the A14 towards Felixstowe and join the A12 at junction 58 after crossing the Orwell Bridge and follow the signs for Woodbridge. You will drive over the railway line just before Woodbridge, this is the location.

There are two lay-bys on this road. Northbound it is to the south of the location on the edge of Martlesham. Southbound is is about 100 metres after the last roundabout in Woodbridge. Failing that there is the Park and Ride or the Tesco store to the south.

2) 20304 heads up the clockwise East Suffolk Line passing under the A12 towards Ipswich with 20305 on the tail.
Photo by Brian Carter, October, 14:45, 160mm

Little Bealings

Location Notes

The location is just to the south of Little Bealings, a quiet country village in the picturesque Fynn Valley, located to the south of Woodbridge on the Suffolk Coast. The crossing is next to the former station buildings which are now rented offices.

1) With the sun setting over the southern hill 37601 and 059 catch the last light of the day on a clockwise RHTT circuit.
   Photo by Calum Hepplewhite, November, 14:45, 95mm

Public Transport

Galloway European, service 70, runs from Ipswich Cattle Market to Woodbridge and calls at Beacon Hill Cross Roads or the Admirals Head Pub Stop and passes over the location but these services are limited to about three a day. Alternatively, First Eastern Counties, service 64, operates hourly between Ipswich Cattle Market and Woodbridge. You should get off in Kesgrave at either the Police Station or Dobbs Lane and walk up Hall Road and The Street to reach the location.

Amenities

There is nothing in the immediate area, the Admirals Head Pub is in Bealings Village. You would need to travel to either Woodbridge or Ipswich for other shops.

Photographic Notes

The favoured shot at this location is of Ipswich bound workings from the southern side of the line. The field edge offers a head-on view of trains approaching the crossing and the field itself a side-on view. Since most workings on the line are limited to 2 or 4 vehicles they should easily fit the frame. Given the specific angle of the shot, the light will be best from late morning to mid afternoon.

The crossing is an automatic half barrier, so it has warbling sirens to warn you of an approaching train. This may be a problem for audio recordings.

Little Bealings

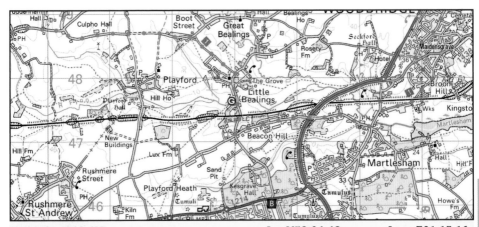

Postcode: IP13 6LT   **Lat N52:04:48**   **Long E01:15:16**

Road Directions

Take the A12 north, past Ipswich, towards Woodbridge. Or take the A14 towards Felixstowe and join the A12 at junction 58 after crossing the Orwell Bridge and follow the signs for Woodbridge until you reach the fourth roundabout and the junction, to the left, with the A1214. Continue along Main Road (A1214) for about ½ a mile and take the right turn onto Hall Road. Drive up the road, going straight over at the crossroads with Martlesham Road and you will reach the location.

There are a couple of field entrances to park at, or the office car parks if spaces are available.

2) With the locally known 'Sizewell Coal' 37423 and 37682 coast past, heading for Ipswich and then on to Willesden.
Photo by Calum Hepplewhite, May, 16:45, 105mm

Westerfield

Location Notes
This is a footpath crossing on the edge of a quiet Suffolk village on the outskirts of Ipswich.

1) Somewhat in need of the carriage washer, 153322 slows for Westerfield before taking the branch to Felixstowe.
February, 10:30, 105mm

Public Transport
National Express, East Anglia, operates an hourly rail service from Ipswich to Westerfield.

Amenities
There is The Railway pub, which is just opposite the station and level crossing. Otherwise it would be back into Ipswich for a wider range of shops.

Photographic Notes
The northern side of the location features steps up a bank with open views in both directions but the southern side is tighter for trains heading towards Felixstowe due to the trees.

The view of Ipswich bound workings is very open as you view across an open area between the foot crossing and the road. This space can sometimes be occupied by vans or materials for permanent way works. The location has a radio mast in the car park which will feature in any east facing shots.

2) With the 20/20 tour the Choppers head to Ipswich.
Photo by Calum Hepplewhite, March, 15:30, dslr@36mm

Anything using the East Suffolk line will need to stop to exchange the RETB token in the station platforms. Workings taking the single track branch to Felixstowe will be travelling slowly past the location taking the crossovers and may even be halted to wait for an Ipswich bound working to pass.

Westerfield

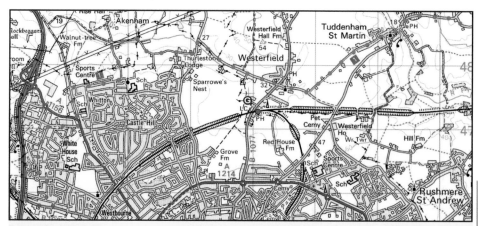

Postcode: IP6 9AE   **Lat N52:04:51**   **Long E01:09:46**

Road Directions

From the north take the A14 and leave at Junction 53, taking the A1156 into Ipswich. After passing the car showroom on your right get into the left feeder lane and turn left at the mini roundabout onto the A1214. Continue past two sets of traffic lights to the roundabout and take the first exit onto Westerfield Road (B1077) and continue until you reach the railway line. From the south leave the A14 at junction 55, taking the A1214. Follow this around Ipswich until you reach Westerfield Road (B1077). Turn left at this roundabout.and continue until you reach the railway line.

Park by the railway line and then walk back down Westerfield Road for about 100 yards and there is a footpath on the right through a field. Take this footpath to the location.

3) On the job training with Freightliner's new acquisition as 70001 powers off the Felixstowe branch towards Ipswich.
Photo by Steve Goodrum, December, 14:45, 75mm

Ipswich, East Suffolk Junction

Location Notes

Located on the western fringe of Ipswich the location is a road bridge. It is on the entrance to a wasteland/ empty lorry trailer storage park. The area is urban housing with light industry around. There are also a number of open areas to the north. Hadleigh Road is quite busy with people walking around and traffic is also heavy.

1) GBRf 66714 rounds the curve with an intermodal, passing the Hadleigh Road 'Gas Tower' in the empty position.
   December, 11:30, 100mm

Public Transport

Ipswich Buses, service 7, operates from Stop 'E' outside the railway station to the Sainsbury's store on Hadleigh Road to the south of the location. On foot it would be about a 20 minute walk from the railway station following Ranelagh Road left out of the station and then crossing straight over the London Road and then following Hadleigh Road up to the bridge.

Amenities

There is a McDonald's at the junction of Hadleigh and London Roads as well as a Sainsbuy's to the south. You are also likely to find 'burger vans' in the Hadleigh Road Industrial Estate.

Photographic Notes

Although this location is fenced off by a large palisade fence the gaps are easily big enough to get still camera lenses through. This, combined with the road noise, would make the location unsuitable for video work.

The Great Eastern line has a large tree growing up behind the fence at about the point where the rear of a loco would

2) 66569 hauls the 'Ipswich Monument' 47370 to Felixstowe.
   Photo by Luke Putland, May, 08:20, 120mm

be. Further back there are lamp posts hindering the view. For East Suffolk traffic the line curves around the industrial estate and a minimum of a 100mm lens will get you over the embankment edges and fencing close to the bridge. The background also features a large gas tower which will dominate the skyline when full. There is a tight shot of Felixstowe bound workings from the southern side of the bridge. The overhead lines part just before the bridge as this is the limit of electrification, giving a clear view.

Ipswich, East Suffolk Junction

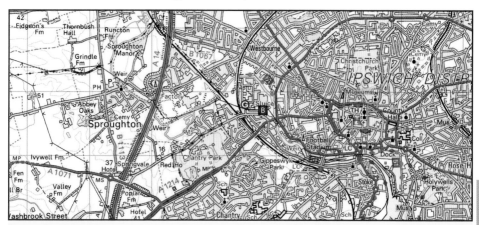

Postcode: IP2 0HP   **Lat N52:03:30**   **Long E01:07:36**

Road Directions

From the A14 J55 or A14/A12 junction follow the A1214 into Ipswich. Once the lanes rejoin, after being separated by an island, you will go down a hill with allotments, behind bushes, on your right. At the traffic lights, before the railway bridge, turn left up Dickens Road. At the end of Dickens Road find somewhere to park and the location is on Hadleigh Road, to the right of the end of Dickens Road.

The entrance to the lorry park is wide and will accommodate 4 or 5 cars on a short term basis when the gates are locked, perhaps at weekends. There is no authorised parking in the industrial estate.

3) With a clockwise RHTT circuit, 20305 and 20304 head south clearing the leaves from the line to Ipswich.
Photo by Brian Carter, October, 15:00, 200mm

Great Eastern Main Line - Norwich to Ipswich

Passenger Traffic

The line hosts both express and local passenger traffic, currently under the National Express East Anglia franchise. Express services run half-hourly between London's Liverpool Street station to Norwich; though hourly on Sundays. Peak time services also work weekdays. These trains are formed of Class 90s at the London-end, Mark III loco-hauled coaching stock, and a DVT at the northern-end of the train. Occasional use is made of hired-in Class 90s from DB Schenker, though this is likely to cease from December 2010 when the timetable is recast.

Class 321 units can often be seen working north of Ipswich in times of service disruption or poor Class 90 availability. Local services can be formed from the Crown Point pool of Class 153, 156 or 170 diesel multiple units.

1) 90035 pushes the 12:30 to Norwich through Mellis.
Photo by Oli Smith, February, , 200mm

Freight Traffic

There is a large amount of intermodal traffic, from Felixstowe, that uses the section between Ipswich and Haughley Junction to gain access to the Bury St Edmunds Line. There is also an amount of aggregate traffic from the terminals at Barham and Ipswich. North of Haughley Junction freight is sparse with only the North Walsham Tanks using the line on a regular basis.

Occasional Traffic

There are often rail tours from Norwich at the weekends, with associated ECS moves usually on the Friday and Monday. These are usually operated by the West Coast Railway Company.

2) 66710 with the North Walsham Tanks, at Swainsthorpe.
Photo by Steve Goodrum, April, 15:45, 75mm

Serco test trains are also regular visitors to the main line, testing both the track and overhead line equipment.

From time to time there are also empty stock movements from Norwich Crown Point depot, sometimes to Ilford in North East London, for tyre turning. These workings produce all sorts of motive power. In the autumn there are the Stowmarket based RHTT trains, which have been operated by Direct Rail Services.

In the event of a train failure there is a 'Thunderbird' based at Colchester in the morning and Shenfield in the afternoon.

3) 37608 leads the Mentor OLE test coach south at Thorpe.
Photo by Steve Goodrum, August, 13:30, 75mm

Great Eastern Main Line - Norwich to Ipswich

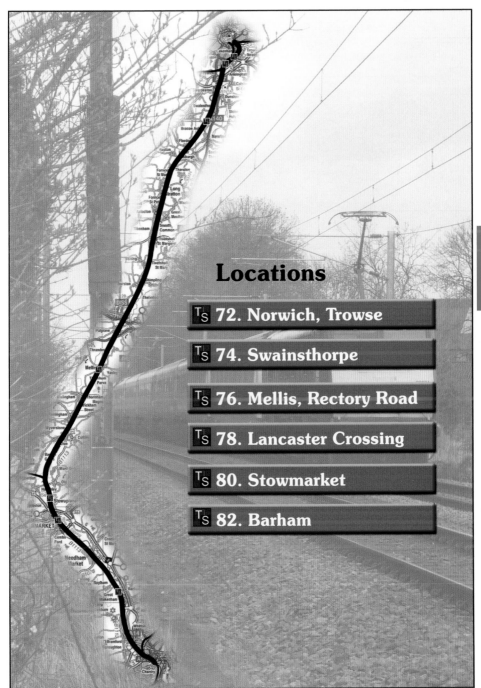

Locations

TS	**72. Norwich, Trowse**
TS	**74. Swainsthorpe**
TS	**76. Mellis, Rectory Road**
TS	**78. Lancaster Crossing**
TS	**80. Stowmarket**
TS	**82. Barham**

Norwich, Thorpe/Trowse

Location Notes

This location is the A146 over bridge, a busy road intersection on the outskirts of Norwich. It crosses the lines to Ely via Thetford and the Great Eastern Main Line to Ipswich and London. The A146 links the Norwich Ring Road (A47) with the south east quarter of Norwich.

1) 20308 heads for Stowmarket with the seasonal RHTT down the GEML.
Photo by Brian Carter, September, 13:00, 150mm

Public Transport

Leave Norwich Station and cross the river on Prince of Wales Road walking for about 10 minutes until you reach the war memorial on Castle Meadow.

First Eastern Counties, service 9, runs between Norwich Castle Meadow to Long John Hill.

From Long John Hill continue south and then turn left and walk along Barrett Road to reach the location.

2) A DVT on the rear of a train to London.
January, 13:30, 55mm

Amenities

There is a BP petrol station just on the right off the A146. On Long John Hill there is the Oasis Stores shop and Long John Fish Bar chip shop.

Photographic Notes

There are options on both the Ely and Great Eastern Main lines from here, although the Norwich bound shots on the GE are a little tight and hindered by the overheads.

For shots of GE London bound traffic you can shoot from the bridge. The line is heading south west and is lit best until early afternoon when the sun will be on the wrong side of the line. The overhead masts are well placed out of shot, or you can climb down the bank to get under the overheads completely. If you do go down the bank mind the horses in the field below.

3) 158812 arrives off the Thetford Line.
January, 14:00, 55mm

For shots of Thetford line traffic the view is open in both directions. This line has options from the north side of the line, so should be available all day.

Norwich, Thorpe/Trowse

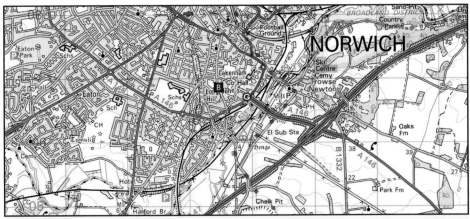

Postcode: NR1 2JA   **Lat N52:36:40**   **Long E01:18:29**

Road Directions

From the A47 follow the A146 signs into Norwich, signposted Trowse County Hall and Football Ground. On the A146 stay in the left hand lane and follow the signs for Cromer A140/Ring Road. You will pass over the lines, and the location. Take the left feeder lane at the junction and continue down the road.

Shortly after the central reservation fence ends you can park on the roadside, on the opposite side of the road.

4) Two Ones with 90012, shoving dead 90014 and a Anglian MkIII set nearing journey's end at Norwich.
Photo by Steve Goodrum, December, 13:00, 150mm

Swainsthorpe

Location Notes

A field location about 3 miles south of Norwich and just north of Swainsthorpe village. The bridge allows a bridleway to cross the line. The area is farmland, the landscape could be described as gently rolling and there are plenty of trees to break up the horizon.

1) Sporting, somewhat dirty, National Express colours, 90009 heads south with a London bound express.
February, 14:00, 55mm

Public Transport

First Eastern Counties, service 18, operates half hourly from the Castle Meadow stop. Simonds, service 2, operates an almost hourly service from the railway station forecourt. Both services will pass the location and you can alight at either Dunston Hall to the north or The Dun Cow to the south and walk for about 10 minutes to the location.

Amenities

There is nothing in the immediate area, with only the Dun Cow pub about a mile to the south on the A140. Norwich would be the best bet for shops.

Photographic Notes

There is no shot from the bridge as the line is very straight and the overhead lines and masts block the view. However the field offers fairly similar shots on both sides. You can pick a height depending on your preference - from around cab height to

2) From the lane 90013 is caught heading south .
Photo by Steve Philpott, September, 10:30, 55mm

below rail level and swap sides when the sun crosses the line, during the early afternoon. For an express the location is about 5 minutes from Norwich.

Although the A140 is just to the east the location is not overly noisy and would be well suited for videographers and audio recordings.

Being field locations you must respect any crops by keeping to the edges.

Swainsthorpe

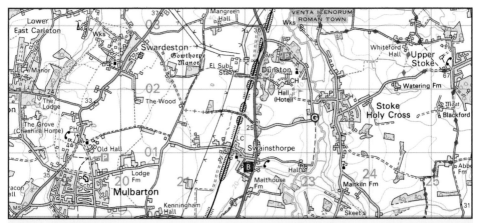

Postcode: NR14 8QB   **Lat N52:34:01**   **Long E01:16:24**

Road Directions

From the A47 take the A140, signed to Ipswich and Diss (A1066), south. After crossing the railway in Dunston you will pass Dunston Hall golf course. Once you break the tree line you will see the railway line and the bridge on your right.

The bridleway turning is on the right, just after the left hand turn into Stoke Lane. It is reasonably wide and is certainly wide enough to allow you to park considerably so that any other vehicles, or farm machinery, can pass. Only farm vehicles would be going to the other side as the bridleway only leads to fields.

3) 70013 heads a 'Cathedrals Express' south after the visit to the Norwich City Cathedral.
Photo by Steve Goodrum, April, 17:45, 75mm

Mellis, Rectory Road

Location Notes

Roughly midway between Diss and Haughley Junction, Mellis is a small Suffolk village. The location is a crossing where the line separates farm buildings and fields.

1) 47802 heads north towards Norwich with a stoneblower destined for testing on the Mid Norfolk at Dereham.
Photo by Oli Smith, June, 16:45, 75mm

Public Transport

Galloway European, service 456, operates two hourly between Diss and Stowmarket. Other than that there are no regular public transport options to the village.

Amenities

The Railway Tavern is a Victorian free house situated in the centre of the village. It serves home cooked food and a good selection of real ales, guest ales changing weekly. It also offers bed and breakfast. Other than that the nearest shops are in Diss, which is about 5 miles to the north.

Photographic Notes

With the line running roughly north east to south west there are shots of southbound workings for most of the day. The locos are usually on the south end of trains, so this would suit 'going away' shots.

The straight nature of the line means shots from the crossing are fairly head on. There is a wider angle for northbound workings but these will only be properly lit during the early part of summer mornings.

The crossing is an automatic half barrier and as such the sirens will warble whenever a train is in the area. Although not very loud this will put off some videographers. They give about 20 seconds warning of an approaching working.

Mellis, Rectory Road

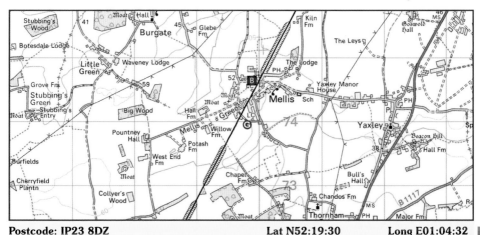

Postcode: IP23 8DZ   **Lat N52:19:30**   **Long E01:04:32**

Road Directions

From Diss: Take the A143 west towards Bury St Edmunds; after about 4 miles you will enter Wortham. Take the road on the left. Follow the sign to Mellis and Yaxley. On the approach to Mellis village you will have to climb a small gradient and at the top is a pair of double bends and on the left hand bend is a single track lane to the right signposted for Gislingham. After approximately 250 yards take the farm track on the left opposite the Church which is on the first bend and the level crossing for this location will be in sight. From the south: take the A14 north from Ipswich and then take the A140 (junction 51) towards Diss. About three miles after the village of Stoke Ash, take the road to the left into the village of Yaxley.In the village, take the left turn into Mellis Road and follow this to the location.

Please be aware this farm track has a very uneven surface and drivers are advised to take care. This is not technically a public highway so be aware of farm machinery using the track. Sufficient parking is available on the concrete pad on the eastern side of the Level Crossing.

2) London bound in the refresher packet colours of 'One' 90007 approaches the crossing at Mellis.
Photo by Luke Putland, July, 17:45, 85mm

Stowmarket, Lancaster Crossing

Location Notes
A foot crossing, in hilly but open farm land, about a mile and a half north of Stowmarket station. To the east is a farm/industrial unit and there are some private houses in the area.

1) Looking west at the Main Line, 90008 heads a London express south towards Stowmarket.
   Photo by Geoff Tibble, November, 09:30, 28mm

Public Transport
First Great Eastern, services 87/88/88A, operate half hourly between Stowmarket and Ipswich. Get off on Chilton Way/Britten Avenue. Turn right on Bury Road and under the A14, then follow the footpaths north to the location.

Amenities
There is a BP Petrol Station about 10 minutes walk away, north west, off Spikes Lane. Otherwise you would be best heading back into Stowmarket.

2) 66540 heads north with for the Bury Line.
   Photo by James Welham, May, 10:30, 110mm

Photographic Notes
Although on a large S-Curve the line runs pretty much north to south through the location. The preferred shot is in the afternoon from the western side of the line. Bushes and banks limit the options for shots from the east side, with only head on or side view shots.

With the exception of the odd bang or crash from the industrial area and the distant drone of the A14 the location is quiet and would be well suited to videographers.

3) 90013 with a lunchtime London bound express.
   Photo by Luke Putland, November, 11:30, 65mm

Stowmarket, Lancaster Crossing

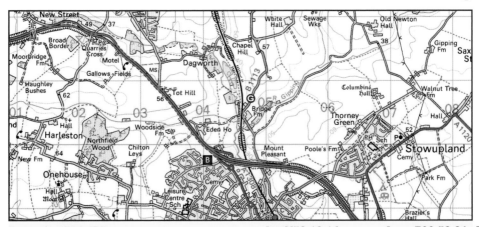

Postcode: IP14 4PD   **Lat N52:12:16**   **Long E00:59:34**

Road Directions

Leave the A14 at Junction 50 and join the A1120 eastbound towards Stowupland village and take the first left onto Stowmarket Road, the B1151. Go under the A14 and straight across the big roundabout. At the mini roundabout turn right and head up Newton Road, going back under the A14 again. After about 2 miles you will reach the location on your left. Park in the lay-by opposite the crossing.

You can also access the location from the A14/A1308 junction and drive down Spikes Lane. But this is a private road and parking is very difficult without blocking the road.

4) Returning to the base at Stowmarket 57003 and 57012 head south with a RHTT working from Norwich
Photo by Oli Smith, November, 15:00, 75mm

Stowmarket

Location Notes

An approach road cul-de-sac to some flats that were, at the time of writing, under construction.

1) Sprinter unit 156419 heads north towards the station with a Cambridge bound National Express local service.
February, 10:30, 90mm

Public Transport

National Express East Anglia operates a regular service to the station from London, Norwich and Ely. Leave the station head and straight out towards the traffic lights. At the lights turn left and follow Gipping Way for around 200 metres, the turning is the second left. Follow this, as yet un-named road down to the location.

Amenities

There are two small shops at the station, at the northern end of Creeting Road, which would be about 5 minutes walk, and Tesco about 15 minutes in the other direction.

Otherwise there are plenty of shops in the town.

2) London bound 90009 pulls away from a stop.
February, 10:30, 50mm

Photographic Notes

The new B1115 relief road in Stowmarket is being built, at the time of writing, over the south of the station. This will divert road traffic away from the level crossing at the north of the station and over the line by means of a bridge. This will impact on the shot, but will mainly remove the trees from the skyline. There is a large radio mast and associated portacabin which is in the middle of a wide angle shot.

A step ladder is not, strictly, necessary as there are roadside barriers on which you can stand to get the extra height.

The road should not have high volumes of traffic, so aside from the general town ambient

3) 37087 arrives in the yard after a hard night's RHTTing.
Photo by Geoff Tibble, November, 08:45, 55mm

noise, audio recordings should be clean, but the radio mast will spoil pan shots for videographers.

Stowmarket

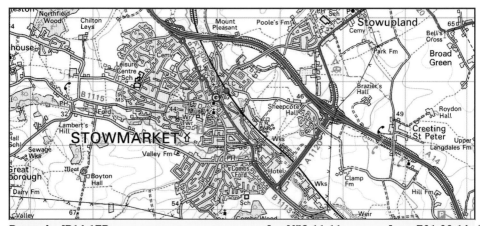

Postcode: IP14 1EP   **Lat N52:11:11**   **Long E01:00:14**

Road Directions

Come off the A14 at junction 50 and follow the A1120 into Stowmarket, straight over the first roundabout opposite Tesco. You will cross over the railway. At the roundabout at the bottom of the road turn right following the A1308 Needham Road/Gipping Way into town. After you pass Hollingsworth Road on your right take the next left and follow this road down to the location.

Currently this road leads to the building site for the new flats. There are a few roadside spaces to park in or you could just park on the road as you will be standing next to your car. It is likely the parking arrangements will change when the flats are constructed, but probably not in any significant manner.

4) This is the Stowmarket base for DRS East Anglian RHTT operations. All of the locos will return here during the day.
Photo by Geoff Tibble, November, 08:30, 155mm

Barham

Location Notes
The location is close to the busy A14 and is an isolated spot. You are surrounded by disused gravel pits which have been landscaped and turned into a wildlife area. There is also a La Farge stone terminal here which has regular traffic.

1) With the La Farge siding in the foreground, DRS 37038 and 57009 head an RHTT south across the foot crossing.
  Photo by David Smith, October, 09:30, 60mm

Public Transport
First Eastern Counties, services 87/88/88A, operate half hourly between Stowmarket and Ipswich Cattle Market. You will need to alight at either the Great Blakenham, Woodfield or Chequers stops and take the footpath to the location.

Amenities
Go back down Penthouse Lane, turn left and 50 yards on the left is the Sorrel Horse pub. Claydon has two pubs and a general stores.

2) 66144 eases past Barham sidings with a working from Mountsorrel.
  Photo by Luke Putland, November, 10:15, 95mm

Photographic Notes
You are fairly close to the line side at the crossing and there are many masts, but walking around the fields will get you scenic shots of passing trains. There are a few mounds of earth that will give you a height advantage on the east of the line.
The area is free from any obvious sources of noise, the quarry facilities are well hidden behind trees, so it would be a good location for videographers.

Barham

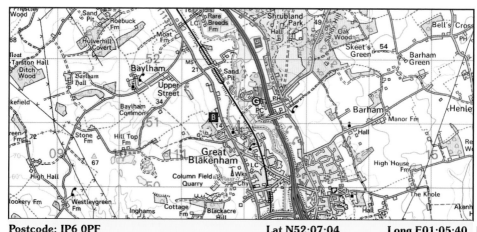

Postcode: IP6 0PF   **Lat N52:07:04**   **Long E01:05:40**

Road Directions

Leave the A14 at junction 52 for Claydon and follow the road through the village. Once you have passed though Cladyon take the next left turn, Pesthouse Road, which leads you back across the A14 onto an access road for the quarry. Park around here.

On the access road you will see a sign stating private property as the land is owned by a fishing club. Whist this is true, there is a public right of way across their land which leads to the location. Follow the electric lines across the park, and between the lakes, to the crossing and the location.

3) One Railway's 90015 hurries a Norwich to London Liverpool Street service south past the stone terminal.
Photo by David Smith, March, 13:30, 95mm

Norwich to Ely - 'Breckland Line'

Passenger Traffic

All of the passenger traffic is operated by Diesel Multiple Units. East Midlands Trains and National Express are the operating companies. A mix of 158 and 170 units provides the cross country traffic.

Freight Traffic

There are only a couple of flows that use the line. These are aggregates working from Norwich to either Peak Forest or Mountsorrel. These run every few days.

Potato traffic was trailed to Eccles Road in 2008 and although there are freight sidings at both Brandon and Eccles Road, which are both active, they have not seen any traffic for a while.

1) 170273 with a Cambridge stopper at Thetford.
February, 12:15, 105mm

Occasional Traffic

The line is used for Empty Coaching Stock moves from the north to Norwich.

During times of major engineering work, or complete closures, on the Great Eastern Main Line, the line can be used as a diversionary route, sets are usually dragged complete with AC traction still attached. From time to time there are also locomotive moves to the Mid Norfolk Railway at Wymondham. This line also provides loading facilities for the Ministry of Defence at Dereham and there is the occasional train that operates to various destinations. The Mid Norfolk also plays host to On Track plant, for testing purposes. So OTP moves are also a possibility.

2) 66141 with a stone working heads for Norwich.
Photo by Geoff Tibble, January. 14:45, 45mm

3) Part of the autumnal preventative maintenance regime of RHTT workings with 20s passing Prickwillow to Norwich.
Photo by Brian Carter, March, 10:45, 120mm

Norwich to Ely - 'Breckland Line'

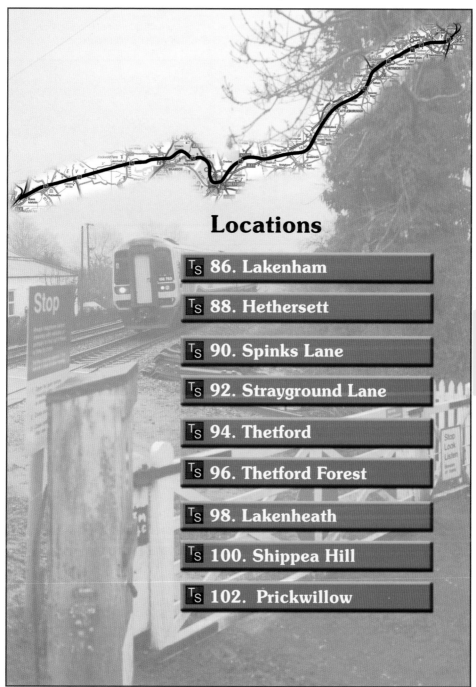

Locations

- ᵀS 86. Lakenham
- ᵀS 88. Hethersett
- ᵀS 90. Spinks Lane
- ᵀS 92. Strayground Lane
- ᵀS 94. Thetford
- ᵀS 96. Thetford Forest
- ᵀS 98. Lakenheath
- ᵀS 100. Shippea Hill
- ᵀS 102. Prickwillow

Lakenham

Location Notes

Lakenham is a suburb of Norwich which covers about a square mile of both the Norwich to Ely and Norwich to London lines once they have passed Trowse Junction, where the two lines part.

1) 37194 powers towards Ely with a Norwich to Long Marston move, conveying 4 MkIII coaches for storage.
Photo by Steve Goodrum, February, 10:00, 150mm

Public Transport

Leave Norwich Station and cross the river on Prince of Wales Road walking for about 10 minutes until you reach the war memorial on Castle Meadow. First Eastern Counties, service 9, runs between Norwich Castle Meadow and Long John Hill.

From Long John Hill continue south and then go straight across the road to Stoke Road, under the GEML, and continue down this road to the location. Anglian Bus & Coach, service 004, runs through the location, but the closest bus stop to the railway station is two thirds of the way to the location.

Amenities

There is The Cock pub on the road to the north of the location. On Long John Hill, just off the main road, there is the Oasis Stores shop and Long John Fish Bar chip shop.

Photographic Notes

There is no pavement on the bridge and bends on either side make it slightly hazardous to anyone

2) 60044 with a short loaded Norwich stone working.
Photo by Jonathan Cordle, September, 12:30, 100mm

standing on it. This is not a location for tripods and great care should be exercised by anyone standing on the bridge. The sides are not high so it is very easy to see over. Shots are available in both directions, but due to vegetation, only from the southern side of the bridge. The GEML can be seen in the background. There are also opportunities from the roadside and fields close to the location.

Lakenham

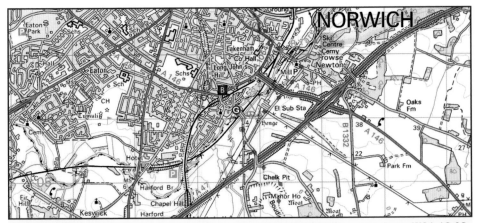

Postcode: NR1 2LZ   **Lat N52:36:23**   **Long W01:18:08**

Road Directions

From the A47 follow the A146 signs into Norwich, signposted Trowse County Hall and Football Ground. On the A146 stay in the left hand lane and follow the signs for Cromer A140/Ring Road. Take the left feeder lane at the junction and continue down the road. Take the first left, down a winding road passing under the Norwich to London mainline, turning left by the Lakenham Cock Inn. Just after turning here is a small space by the side of the road to park.

3) A4 60009, taking the Breckland route, departs Norwich with a charter to Scarborough.
Photo by Chris Nesbitt, July, 06:15, 70mm

Hethersett

Location Notes

Just off the busy A11 this is a road bridge joining the A11 with East Carleton, to the south of the village of Hethersett. It is opposite the site of the former station and Oil Depot that used to serve RAF Coltishall until the air base was closed in 2006.

There will be very few people walking past but there will be plenty of traffic passing by.

1) Passing the former station, and former oil sidings behind the chimney, 37601 heads towards Ely with a RHTT.
Photo by Jonathan Cordle, November, 11:15, 160mm

Public Transport

Take a bus from Norwich rail station to the bus station then First Eastern Counties, service 15A from Norwich bus station to Hethersett, Colney Lane. From there it is about a 10 minute walk to the location.

Amenities

The Thickthorn Services are about ½ a mile away on A11.

Photographic Notes

The bridge offers excellent views in both directions. The location will be well lit from mid morning until the early evening, depending on direction. The sides of the bridge are a little high and a step ladder certainly would be useful, but not essential. Visibility in the opposite direction is difficult. The A11 provides a constant drone of noise that will interfere with any audio recordings, making it unsuitable for videographers.

2) 20310 and 20313 top and tail a westbound RHTT.
Photo by Jonathan Cordle, December, 11:15, 105mm

Hethersett

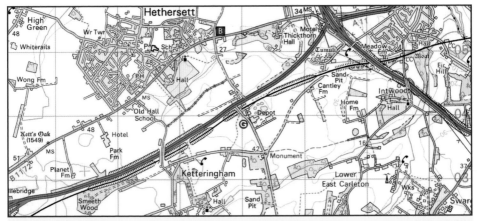

Postcode: NR9 3AZ   **Lat N52:35:28**   **Long E01:12:05**

Road Directions

From the A47 Norwich Ring Road: leave at the junction for Thickthorn Services and follow the A11 south, signed to Thetford and London. Do not follow the signs for Hethersett Village.

After about ½ a mile take the left turn, just before a 'Telephone 250m' sign onto Station Lane and you will drive over the location.

There are many roadside grass verges on which you can park.

3) With the final stage of a Stowmarket to Norwich, via Ely, working, 37087 and 37601 clear the tracks at Hethersett.
Photo by Jonathan Cordle, November, 10:30, 75mm

Wymondham, Spinks Lane

Location Notes

This is a gated country lane crossing on a little used road. The ends of the road join junctions of the A11 so it will only be the odd farm vehicle passing by.

Public Transport

First Eastern Counties, service 13, runs hourly from Norwich bus station to the Waitrose at Wymondham, with two early morning services calling at the Business Park which is slightly closer to the location. From Waitrose it will be about a 20 minute walk to the location.

The location is also about a 20 minute walk from Wymondham station, which has an hourly service from Norwich or Cambridge.

Amenities

There is nothing at the location, but Wymondham has a wide range of shops and take-aways.

1) A Cambridge bound 170272 approaches the crossing.
February, 09:45, 105mm

Photographic Notes

The crossing is a 'red and green' type, meaning there are small 'traffic lights' indicating an approaching train. This combined with clicking within relay boxes gives plenty of notice of approaching workings. To the west is a signal protecting a crossing, which is usually amber. When this clears to green the crossing is down and the train is likely to be westbound.

There are mounds of earth on both sides of the crossing where you could stand, but a telephoto lens would be required to get past the crossing signage.

The banks and trees around the crossing are quite high and will throw shadows across the line,

2) The sign makes the crossing location apparent, telephoto lens required.
February, 09:45, 105mm

particularly for westbound workings.

Although the A11 is about ½ a mile away, the location is very quiet. Combined with the dead straight nature of the line it would make for a good video location, but watch out for the signs.

Wymondham, Spinks Lane

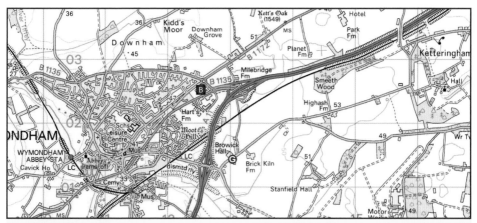

Postcode: NR18 9RA   **Lat N52:34:31**   **Long E01:08:38**

Road Directions

From the northern A11 exit to Wymondham: the lane is an unmarked exit from the roundabout if you are coming off the eastbound carriage way. From the westbound direction you will need to head into Wymondham turn back to the A11, towards Norwich, leave the A11 on the slip road leading to the B1135, then turn right on the B1135 and go under the A11. Go straight across the roundabout onto Spinks Lane. The lane is wide enough for one car to pass another, but it is best to leave space in case farm machinery needs to get past.

3) Heading up a Wroxham bound charter 66078 heads east towards Norwich.
Photo by Calum Hepplewhite, September, 10:45, 185mm

Wymondham, Strayground Lane

Location Notes

A manually operated gate crossing just to the south west of Wymondham station. The lane is essentially a dead end, leading to a few private dwellings and fields to the south of the line.

Public Transport

Wymondham station has an hourly service from Norwich or Cambridge.
Leave the station and turn left up Cemetery Lane. Just up the lane is a foot crossing over the connection to the Mid Norfolk Railway which you should cross and then turn left and continue down Strayground Lane to the location.

Amenities

There is nothing in the immediate area. The industrial area has a number of burger vans and Wymondham town has plenty of shops

Photographic Notes

The location has a couple of semaphores, operated from Wymondham box, just around the corner. These give ample warning and directional indication, of approaching workings.

The southern side of the crossing is very restricted in its view and as such is pretty unusable but the northern side offers views in both directions. For Norwich bound workings the line curves in and would suit telephoto lens shots. Or you can shoot from the hill to give you a range of heights over the crossing. This area appears to be wasteland and in the summer would become quite overgrown, so clippers might be useful.

The location is far from any obtrusive sources of noise, the recycling centre up the lane may provide the odd clank. There is plenty of space for tripods so the location is well suited to videographers.

1) Changing the oil lamps on the peg as 170270 passes.
February, 10:45, 50mm

2) Norwich bound 170270 slows for a station stop.
February, 10:15, 90mm

3) 158788 on the crossing with an express to Norwich.
February, 10:15, 90mm

Wymondham, Strayground Lane

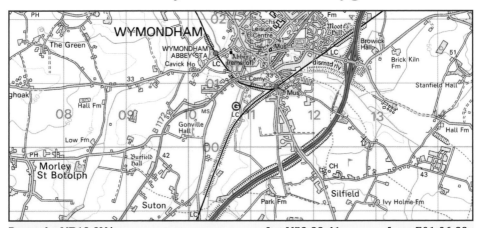

Postcode: NR18 9NA   **Lat N52:33:41**   **Long E01:06:33**

Road Directions

From the A11 take the exit signed to 'Wymondham Industrial Estate' and once you have crossed over the railway line take the first exit at the roundabout into the industrial area. At the end of the industrial area, opposite a big blue children's play area building, turn right. At the traffic lights turn left along the B1172 following the signs to Attleborough. After you cross the railway bridge take the next left (Whartons Lane), opposite the fire station, then the first left into Strayground Lane and continue to the location.

You can park your car on the lane but be prepared to move if anyone needs to use the crossing.

4) Shortly before the telegraph wires and poles were removed 20311 and 20312 top and tail an Ely bound RHTT.
Photo by Jonathan Cordle, November, 12:15, 105mm

Thetford, Woodlands Footbridge

Location Notes

This is a footbridge over the line between two residential estates. The area has a lot of people passing, either across the line or along the path parallel to the line.

1) With a Norwich bound EMT working, 158783 accelerates away from a station stop just before the peg is reset.
February, 12:15, 105mm

Public Transport

Thetford is well served by rail from Norwich, Cambridge and the Midlands. The location is about a 20 minute walk from the station.

Thetford Coach Services, T2, also goes from the leisure centre to Shelly Way, from where you can access the location. But as the service is hourly it would, usually, be quicker to walk.

Amenities

There is nothing at the location. There are a chip shop and newsagents opposite the turning to Woodland Drive about 5 to 10 minutes walk away along with some more shops on Admirals Way to the south.

Photographic Notes

The line runs north east to south west and Ely bound workings will be well lit from early morning to mid afternoon. The bridge is well

2) Westbound 158799 slows on the approach to the station.
February, 12:30, 55mm

raised over the line and there is little to throw shadows on the southern side of the line. The bridge sides are not high so a step ladder is not required. The location is close to some schools so, at certain times of day, there will be lots of screaming noise in the background. However, aside from that, the location is reasonably quiet making it quite suitable for video, but the bridge is fairly narrow so tripods should be used with consideration for the passing public.

Thetford, Woodlands Footbridge

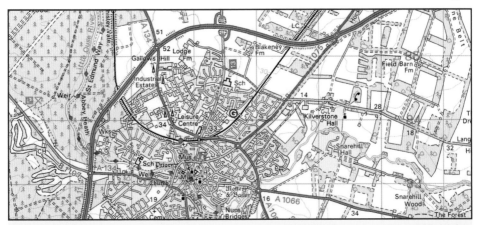

Postcode: IP24 1UE   **Lat N52:25:21**   **Long E00:45:34**

Road Directions

From the A11 take the Croxton exit, a turning between the A1066 and A1075 roundabouts and head south into Thetford. Just after passing the school on your left, turn left into Woodlands Drive and follow this road all the way round to the location.

There are plenty of roadside parking places.

3) The telegraph poles have gone but the Breckland RHTT still runs, seen here with 37069 leading into Thetford.
Photo by Brian Carter, October, 10:15, 200mm

Thetford Forest, Santon

Location Notes
This location is in the middle of Thetford Forest, well away from any built-up area. In the summer it is often quite busy with families on a day out. The level crossing is referred to as 'Santon' on the railway.

1) A4 60019 heads through the Thetford Forest with a Norwich charter. The telegraph pole has since been removed.
Photo by Geoff Tibble, May, 14:15:, 60mm

Public Transport
There is no public transport to the location but Brandon is about 3 miles away - there are plenty of well signposted forest walks, some of which are parallel to the railway.

Amenities
There are public toilets here, but nothing else. The nearest shops are at Brandon, about 3 miles away, including take-aways and a small supermarket.

Photographic Notes
The line runs approximately north west to south east here and shots are best for Norwich bound trains from mid morning onwards, with the sun on the nose until around 14:00.

2) 66178 heads east on charter towards the crossing.
Photo by Nick Slocombe, May, 14:15:, 105mm

Shots of eastbound trains are also possible from near the level crossing, after the St Helens picnic area turn. Either shoot from the crossing itself, or walk 100 yards or more eastwards between the trees and the fence. A step ladder will be very useful for this shot but note that because the line curves from the left, the back of long trains will be lost from the frame. The sun remains on the nose for longer here than at the picnic area, but shadows from trees are more of a problem.

There is plenty of warning of approaching trains as they can be heard shortly after leaving or passing through Brandon - the sound travels far in the forest. Both locations would be suitable for video with only the sounds of the forest and the occasional USAF jet fighter to add to the sound track.

Thetford Forest, Santon

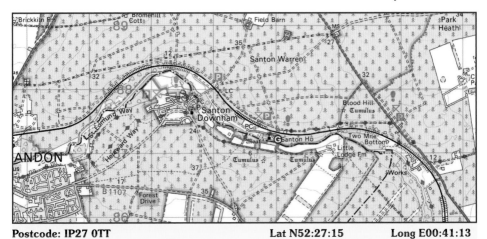

| Postcode: IP27 0TT | Lat N52:27:15 | Long E00:41:13 |

Road Directions

From the A11 in Thetford, take the B1107, towards Brandon, forking right after a mile or so to follow the signs towards Santon Downham. Once in Santon, follow the sign to the 'Forestry Commission - East of England Office'. Just after crossing a narrow iron white arch bridge turn right and follow this road to the signposted St Helens picnic area.

On entering the picnic area, keep to the left and park in the left hand corner close to the railway line. Walk westwards through the trees into the open field. At the time of writing there was no car parking charge, but there is a ticket machine that has been covered over, out of use, for many years.

3) 37605 and 37606 growl through the forest with a Derby to Norwich overhead line test train move.
Photo by Oli Smith, August, 15:15, 75mm

Lakenheath

Location Notes
This location is in fields and farm land, with various level crossings, to the east of Lakenheath station.

1) 170638 heads westbound on the approach to Lakenheath Station.
Photo by Brian Carter, Feb, 16:30, 135mm

Public Transport
Lakenheath station is a request stop on the Cambridge to Norwich route, with only random weekend services booked to stop.
It would be best to check with the train revenue protection officer or the guard before travelling.

Amenities
There is nothing in the immediate area, but Walkers snack bar, back on the A11 is highly recommended. You may also find a 'burger van' at the Lakenheath air base viewing area

Photographic Notes
The line runs roughly east to west and will have options for most of the day, depending on direction. There is little in the way of trees to throw shadows on the line.
There are no sources of industrial noise in the area. but the location is a few miles from Lakenheath USAF air base and the noise of jet fighters is frequent and often very loud.
The semaphores protecting the crossing will raise when there is a train due, giving plenty of notice and a clue as to the direction of travel.
Please be respectful of any crops in the fields.

2) 20309 and 312 warble an RHTT set west to Ely.
Photo by Paul Davis, November, 11:45, 180mm

3) Departing the station 170273 heads to Norwich.
Photo by Paul Davis, November, 11:45, 65mm

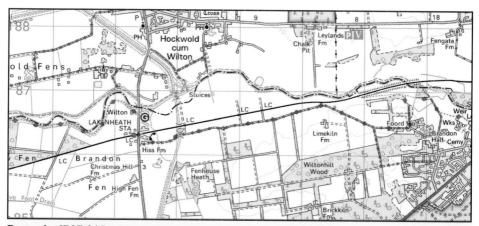

Postcode: IP27 9AD   **Lat N52:26:52**   **Long E00:32:19**

Road Directions

From the A11 at the Barton Mills roundabout follow the A1065 towards Brandon, passing the excellent Walkers snack bar on the right.

Continue through Lakenheath, passing the air base on your left. Just after the air base there are some traffic lights with a left turn to the viewing area, take this but continue past the viewing area. At the end of the road turn right, following the signs to Hockwold and Feltwell, **not** to Lakenheath. As you approach the station you will see some farm buildings with a right turn just before them. Take this turn and head along this bumpy lane/farm track picking your location as required.

When you park, bear in mind that large farm machinery uses this lane so leave space accordingly.

4) Heading towards Norwich a pair of 20s top and tail on the Breckland RHTT circuit.
Photo by Brian Carter, October 10:30, 200mm

Shippea Hill

Location notes

In the middle of nowhere in Cambridgeshire this location is roadside or field edges to the west of the station. The station has been called 'One of the least-used railway stations' in the country.

1) 158813 speeds eastwards, past the crossing and station, towards Thetford and on to Norwich.
February, 14:30, 65mm

Public transport

Shippea Hill station is a request stop on the Cambridge to Norwich route, with only random weekend services booked to stop. It would be best to check with the train revenue protection officer, or the guard, before travelling.

Amenities

There is nothing near the location, with the closest civilisation being around Ely.

Photographic notes

The line is dead straight for many miles around the location. The field edges offer many places to shoot from, but with the line on an embankment it is best suited to shots from the southern side of the line.

To access the field you need to cross a rickety bridge so tread carefully. If you want to get to the fields to the north of the line you will have to walk up the road and back down to get over the stream.

2) 66012 west, towards Ely, with Peak Forest stone empties.
February, 14:15, 55mm

The location might suffer from the noise of traffic waiting pass over the crossing but once in the field the only problem would be wind noise, or the odd jet fighter.

Shippea Hill

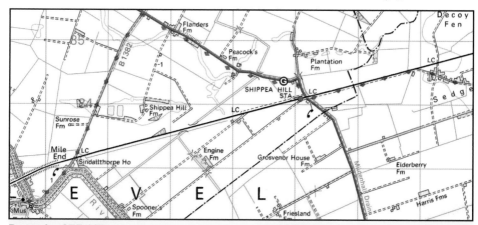

Postcode: CB7 4SP   **Lat N52:25:49**   **Long E00:24:48**

Road Directions

Shippea Hill is mid way on the A1101. This road joins the A10 at Littleport to the north and the A11 at the Barton Mills roundabout to the south.

From the A10, leave at the roundabout at Littleport follow the signs towards Mildenhall and Sedge Fen and you will reach the location.

From the A11, leave at the Barton Mills roundabout and continue towards Mildenhall, which you will pass on your left, and continue until you reach the location.

Once there you can park in the station car park.

3) With the rickety bridge in the foreground 47818 hauls 86238 towards Ely during the Ipswich tunnel blockade.
Photo by Brian Carter, July, 13:00, 135mm

Prickwillow

Location Notes
Approximately midway between Ely and Shippea Hill stations, this is a quiet Fenland location, offering a choice of panoramic views of the Cambridgeshire countryside.

1) With Ely cathedral poking up on the horizon 70013 heads a charter east, bound for Norwich.
Photo by Geoff Tibble, August, 12:30, 70mm

Public Transport
With only one bus a day there and back, there is no viable option for public transport, other than a half hour walk from Queen Adelaide.

Amenities
There is nothing near the location, with the closest shops being in Ely.

Photographic Notes
The occupation crossings offer a variety of long straight shots of trains approaching in either direction. Anything looking towards Ely will have the power lines dominating the skyline.

The line is also a climb from Ely so all workings should be powering.

From the level crossing, or from parts of the roadside, you have various panoramic options. The level crossing is an automatic half barrier so it does have warbling sirens but these were noticeably soft at the time of writing. There is plenty of space so all the locations would be well suited for videographers

2) 47813 heads a DBSO east with a drag to Norwich.
Photo by Brian Carter, July, 13:00, 85mm

3) 47760 leads a charter from Norwich towards Ely.
Photo by Geoff Tibble, August, 12:30, 60mm

Prickwillow

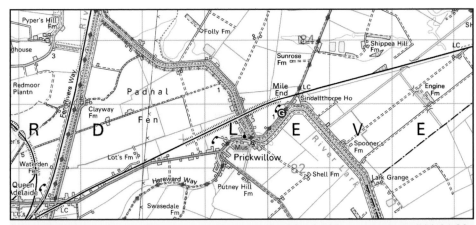

Postcode: CB7 4SJ   **Lat N52:25:22**   **Long E00:21:30**

Road Directions

From the south follow the signs towards Ely Station. When you reach the roundabout opposite Tesco continue along the road to the next roundabout and turn right heading under the railway line. Cross the river and then take the next left and follow this road for about 1½ miles. You will pass under the Norwich line and arrive at the crossroads in Queen Adelaide village.

Approaching from the North on the A10: at the Littleport Roundabout with the A1101 continue straight across the roundabout down the road that runs parallel to the river on it's east side. After several miles you will reach Queen Adelaide village.

From Queen Adelaide head east on the B1382 which is signposted to Prickwillow. The crossings are visible across the fields and if you continue along this road you will pass over the level crossing. There is an area of hard standing just after the crossing on the left.

4) A full 'One' Anglia rake of stock with 47714 on the front and 88225 on the rear approaches the level crossing.
Photo by Paul Davis, July, 14:00, 200mm

Ely to Peterborough

Passenger Traffic

A mixture of operators use the line. East Midlands Trains workings to Norwich, usually with 158s, National Express East Anglia workings to Ipswich, with a mix of 170s and 156s. Cross Country also operate from Derby to Stanstead Airport using 170s.

Freight Traffic

There are plenty of cross country intermodals to Felixstowe from Freightliner, GBRf and DB Schenker. Although the class 66s currenlty hold the traction monopoly, Freightliner class 70s are expected to appear in 2010.

There are also regular aggregate flows, operated by Freightliner and DB Schenker, to the region's stone terminals in Barham, Norwich, Broxbourne and Middleton Towers. In preparation for the 2012 Olympics there are various construction flows. Colas operates a single flow between West Burton and Tilbury for Cemex, which can produce either 66s or 47s. DB Schenker operates the Plasmor 'Blocks' to Bow Olympic.

Occasional Traffic

The line is a diversionary route for the East Coast Main Line. In the event of engineering work between Peterborough and Hitchin workings are, on occasional weekends, diverted this way. This will be either HSTs or 180s as the MkIV stock is not cleared for the line.

There are a number of stock moves, either loco hauled stock or weekend railtours or National Express stock returning from overhaul.

Whitemoor traffic is far from occasional but it does not follow any specific, month in month out, schedule. It is currently the base for one of Network Rail's High Output Ballast Cleaners, or HOBC, trains. When fully formed it is over half a mile long with top and tailed 66s, currently provided by Freightliner Heavy Haul. But the yard also provides infrastructure trains for the Anglia region, the Midlands and some parts of

1) XC 170638 heads towards March on a Stansted trip.
Photo by Brian Carter, June, 11:15, 50mm

2) 66594 on a lightly loaded Felixstowe bound intermodal .
Photo by Rob Brooks, March, 12:30, 130mm

3) 66703 departs Whitemoor with a 'to be filled' spoil train.
Photo by Brian Carter, March, 11:45, 55mm

London. There are frequent ballast workings, spoil trains and track and sleeper movements. These will run from either direction. There are also frequent reversing movements east from the yard so a train can be turned on the Ely Loop and then back into Whitemoor.

GBRf has regular locomotive moves from its Peterborough base to the yard. This has been known to bring the yard pilot, a class 73, out on the main line.

Ely to Peterborough

Locations

T_S 106. Welney Washes

T_S 108. Manea

T_S 110. Westry

T_S 112. March Triangle Bridges

T_S 114. March, Silt Drove

T_S 116. Turves, Beggars' Bridge

T_S 118. Whittlesea, Hearts Drove

T_S 120. Black Bush and Ramsey Rd

Welney Washes

Location Notes

A large viaduct and bridge where the line crosses what are known as the Hundred Foot Washes - two man-made rivers (the Old Bedford River and New Bedford River, also known as the Hundred Foot Drain) with a flood plain in between. Built as a cut off for the River Great Ouse, avoiding Ely, it has become a nature reserve and regularly floods in winter. As you are on a river bank in a very flat area you are open to all the wind and have no shelter, other than under the rail bridge. There is plenty of bird life to be seen in the area and some military aircraft from the numerous Suffolk air bases.

1) An unidentified 170 provides the silhouette as it crosses the Washes with the setting winter sun.
Photo by Brain Carter, November, 15:45, 50mm

Public Transport

There are two buses, running once a day, that pass the location or serve villages nearby but given the frequency and distance to the location, these options are not really viable.

Amenities

There are no toilet facilities in the area, the nearest would be in either Littleport or Ely or the pubs in Little Downham and Welney.

Photographic Notes

The line runs north west to south east, with the primary shot of eastbound workings. The sun will be on the north side of the line early in the morning, crossing to the south side mid morning until mid afternoon.

2) On a late running Peak Forest stone, 60021 heads east.
Photo by Brian Carter, October, 09:00, 50mm

It is possible to shoot trains heading the other way, but the view is not especially good. In the winter, sunset and silhouette shots are possible from the north side of the line.

When the washes are flooded (a regular occurrence in winter), various reflection shots are possible. Videographers could get some good shots here. Trains are visible approaching from the west for some time and there is only the wind to interfere with the audio at this very exposed location.

Welney Washes

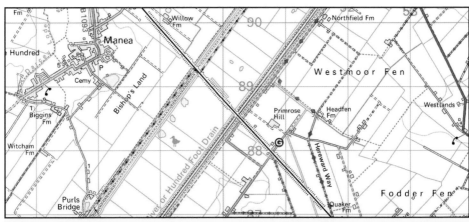

Postcode: CB6 2EH   **Lat N52:28:25**   **Long E00:12:41**

Road Directions

From the A10, Ely By Pass, take the B1411 via Little Downham and Pymore. The road turns left at Pymore and then right at the river. The location is along the river bank.

From the A141 at March, follow the signs to Manea. Continue through Manea Village along the B1093 towards, and then through, Welney Village. After crossing all three Drains, turn right at the T junction on the B1101. About a mile down, the road curves to the left, ignore this and continue straight along what is now the B1411 to reach the location.

Once there you can park your car off-road on the bank.

3) 47712 leads 47709 on the Blue Pullman's initial outing, a circular trip round the Fens from Kings Cross.
Photo by Albert Dawson, January, 15:00, 45mm

Manea, Welney Road Crossing

Location Notes

This location is in open fields, close to an automatic half barrier level crossing just to the east of Manea station.

1) With a short section of the HOBC, 66514 heads a westbound maintenance move from West Ealing to March.
Photo by Brian Carter, September, 16:30, 50mm

Public Transport

Manea Station is served by an hourly service from Ely from where it will be a 10 minute walk.

Amenities

There is a chip shop and a few other shops in Manea village, about ¾ of a mile away.

Photographic Notes

The line runs north west to south east, over very flat fenlands. By looking at the semaphore signals, visible at the level crossing to the west, you can deduce which direction a train is coming from, and you can also see the level crossing barriers at Manea station.

Lineside vegetation and the radio cabin make westbound shots from the northern side difficult. But from the south well lit shots are possible in both directions from mid morning until the end of daylight

2) Mimicking the ECML GC and HT workings pass.
Photo by Brian Carter, March, 17:15, 50mm

- there are no problems with shadows. There are a few lineside bushes which may affect shots. For videographers the crossing does have warbling sirens but the road is very quiet, so traffic noise should be unlikely. The crossing itself has a large radio mast and cabin which is an ugly structure, but this is on the north side of the line and the cabin should be obscured by the train during pans.

Manea, Welney Road Crossing

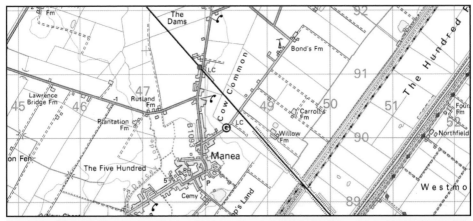

Postcode: PE15 0GR   **Lat N52:29:29**   **Long E00:11:11**

Road Directions

From the south take the A142 west out of Ely towards Chatteris and after about 5 miles turn right onto the B1098. Follow the signs to Manea Station, continue over the railway and take the next left to the location. From the west follow the A141 south through March and then take the left turn onto the B1093 in Wimblington. Follow the signs to Manea Station and when you arrive in Manea turn right and then take the next left up to the location..

3) 66532 heads through the chilly Fens towards Felixstowe with an intermodal with some very cold goods.
Photo by Brian Carter, December, 12:00, 50mm

Westry

Location Notes

Just to the west of March station and Whitemoor Yard, this area is open farmland on the edge of the town. The A141 bridge is one of the few bridges over the railway between Peterborough and Ely. The road is quite busy as it is a trunk route through the Fens. There is a footway on both sides of the road but few pedestrians pass. The surrounding fields are quiet.

1) With the A141 bridge behind, 66526 & the HOBC head west across the fen, catching the last rays of the setting sun.
Photo by Allan Sibley, May, 20:45, 120mm

Public Transport

Take a bus from the station to the local Tesco and walk back to the location. The location is about ½ a mile before the supermarket. You will have crossed the bridge to get to Tesco.

The field location is a 5 minute walk continuing south to the roundabout and then left up Whitemoor Road.

Amenities

To the north of the road bridge there is a Tesco supermarket and fuel station. March town centre has plenty of other shops, including places to eat.

Photographic Notes

There is plenty of notice of approaching workings. To the west is a level crossing where you will see the barriers dropping for an approaching train. To the east you can see for many miles.

The shot of westbound trains requires a telephoto lens, due to tall trees on the southern side of the line, which restrict the angle slightly and cast shadows.

2) 60097 leaves March westbound on stone empties for Peak Forest.
Photo by James Welham, May, 12:30, dslr@300mm

On both sides there are large pavement areas so it is quite safe, but crossing the busy road is not something to do without care. The bridge sides are about 5 feet high so a step ladder may be a bonus, especially as it will allow you to see both directions.

The bridge vibrates with passing road traffic. This, combined with the noise, would be a major problem for videographers and audio recordings.

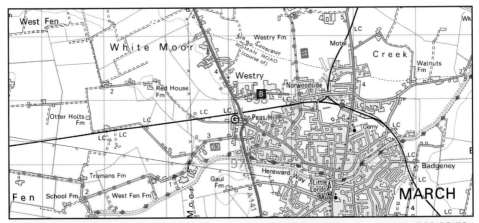

Postcode: PE15 0ER   **Lat N52:33:36**   **Long E00:03:59**

Road Directions

The A141 is the main road between Huntingdon (A1) and Wisbech (A47). The location is on the A141 just to the north of March. If approaching from the Ely direction take the A142 towards Chatteris. This joins the A141 at Chatteris. Take the A141 to March.

You can park near the bridge to the north in a large road turning, but this can be used by farm machinery to access the fields. Tesco's car park is the other option.

3) 56117 with a short enterprise working, back when these existed, heads east towards the yards at Whitemoor.
Photo by Brian Carter, April, 11:30, 80mm

March Triangle Bridges

Location Notes

These locations are bridges around the triangle for March Whitemoor Yard. The footbridge is over the main line and the road bridge is on the yard throat. Both bridges are regularly used by pedestrians.

1) Far from the 3rd rail, GBRf's 73207 performs a shunt move with the HOBC as seen from Norwood Road bridge.
Photo by Brian Carter, July, 10:30, 50mm

Public Transport

March is well served by services from Peterborough and Cambridge. The footbridge is about 5 minutes walk from March Rail Station.

Amenities

Norwood Road has a small store for light snacks and refreshments. There are also many shops in March town centre and Tesco to the west.

Photographic Notes

The footbridge is on a gentle curve coming out of March Station. Offering shots in both directions there should be options for most of the day with only a large portacabin making west facing shots from the north of the footbridge unviable.

The footbridge is of lattice construction and the Norwood Road bridge is reasonably low sided so no step ladder would be required at either bridge.

2) 67029 pushes the the DBS company train east.
Photo by Brian Carter, May, 15:45, 50mm

The Norwood Road Bridge offers views of yard shunting movements and departures. The line on the left, viewed from Norwood Road, is a headshunt so all departures would be on the right hand lines and the view will be compromised by the yard lights. The points should give clues as to the departure direction. The other line heading straight off to the north is the currently mothballed route to Wisbech which may see some freight use in the future.

March Triangle Bridges

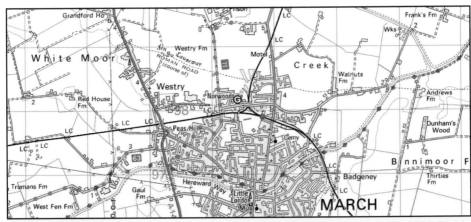

Postcode: PE15 8NY   **Lat N52:33:41**   **Long E00:05:11**

Road Directions

From the A141 to the west of March, take the A1099 into March and just after the 30mph limit commences, there is a mini roundabout. Turn left here and continue along Norwood Road, over the railway. Take the right turn signposted Norwood Road Industrial Area. You will pass Locomotive Drive on your left, this is the site of the original March depot.

Park somewhere, roadside, on Norwood Road and continue on foot as the car parks are now for residents only and the restaurant car park is for patrons only.

The footpath to the bridge is opposite the pub/Cantonese restaurant, between the fences. The bridge for views of the yard is further along Norwood Road.

3) Grand Central route learner and passenger diversion with 43080 at the helm heads east towards March Station.
Photo by Brian Carter, March, 10:15, 50mm

March, Silt Drove

Location Notes
A small road crossing on the western outskirts of March. The line is on a raised embankment with the road joining some houses to the north with the town.

1) Lit by the early morning sun, a southbound shot of 60059 approaching the crossing with a Peak Forest stone.
Photo by Peter Foster, June, 07:30, 100mm

Public Transport
Between 10:00 and 18:00 Stagecoach, service 33, operates from March Station to South Drive from where it is a short walk to the location.

Amenities
There is a small village store on Upwell Road to the south of the location. Other than that March has plenty of shops and take aways.

Photographic Notes
The line is a large 'S' curve heading south out of March, raised up on an embankment. There are only a few bushes that would cast shadows when the sun drops down low. The north to south nature of the line favours workings heading towards Ely with these shots being on from early morning to later afternoon. After that the sun would be round far enough for Peterborough workings.

The crossing fence and the style on the footpath can also offer a height boost if required.

The barriers on the Badgeney crossing lowering will give notice of approaching workings.

There are no major sources of noise in the area and the road up to the crossing has plenty of room for tripods making this location idea for videographers.

2) With a cross country intermodal 66954 heads to Ely.
Photo by Geoff Tibble, month, xx:xx:, 400mm

3) 43084 tails a diverted GC working towards Ely.
Photo by Geoff Tibble, March, 15:30, 55mm

March, Silt Drove

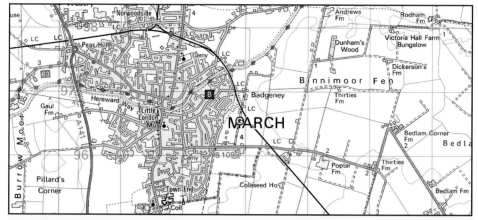

Postcode: PE15 0DB   **Lat N52:32:59**   **Long E00:06:23**

Road Directions

From the Mill Hill Roundabout to the south of March town which is the junction of the A141 and B1101, take the B1101 north. At the junction with the B1099 turn right, signposted Cemetery, out of March passing the Rose and Crown Pub and continue along St Peters Road. Just before the national speed limit signs there is a narrow, well hidden, left hand turning which is Silt Road which leads to the crossing.

You may prefer to drive across the line and park on the northern side as there is little room for cars to pass on the southern side.

4) With a York to Stowmarket RHTT wagon positioning move, 37059 accelerates out of March heading to Ely.
Photo by Peter Foster, September, 14:00, 100mm

Turves, Beggars' Bridge

Location Notes
A Cambridgeshire bridge, known as Beggars' Bridge, across a dyke deep in the Fens. The location is very exposed to the elements.

1) Reflecting in the Twenty Foot River a Cross Country 170 speeds west towards Whittlsea and then Peterborough.
Photo by Jon Bradley, September, 11:30, 50mm

Public Transport
Stagecoach, service 33, operates between Peterborough, Whittlesey and March. The service runs either hourly or half hourly in the middle of the day. You will need to alight at the Coates, Eldernell Lane stop and walk for approximately 10 minutes to reach the location.

Amenities
None at the location, the closest shops are in Whittlesey about 2 miles away.

Photographic Notes
The flat nature of the fenlands means that approaching trains can be seen for a great distance. The track is slightly elevated relative to the road position. The location is fine for any time of day as there is very little to cast shadows in any direction. The shot of westbound trains from the western bank is spoiled by trees and electricity masts but you can get good westbound shots from the east bank, but then eastbound shots wouldn't feature the river. It will just be a case of choosing your preferred side before the working arrives.

The wind can be very obtrusive so adequate wind shielding is a must but there is little else to interfere with audio recordings.

2) GBRf 66724 heads east towards Peterborough.
Photo by Brian Carter, May, 14:45, 50mm

3) 158847 heads east towards an icy March.
Photo by James Welham, January, 12:00, 55mm

Turves, Beggars' Bridge

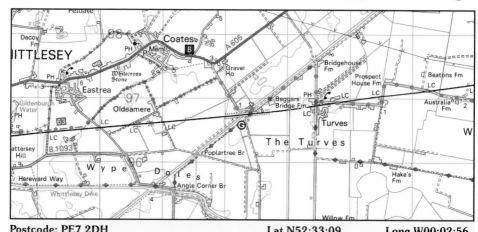

Postcode: PE7 2DH   **Lat N52:33:09**   **Long W00:02:56**

Road Directions

From the Peterborough Ring Road (A1139) leave at either junction 3a or 4, which is opposite the large Ikea distribution centre and take the A605 Peterborough Road out of town. Continue through Whittlsey to the village of Coates. After Coates village, near where the 40mph speed limit starts, take the turning on the right signposted 'Turves / Packing Station' and continue down the road to the location. You will need to turn under the bridge, a blue 63 cycle route sign denotes the turn.

Once under the bridge park on the grass verge. There is off road parking for a number of cars.

4) With a Network Rail Civil engineers spoil train 66097 returns to Whitemoor yard after a hard days night.
Photo by Jon Bradley, September, 11:00, 30mm

Whittlesea, Hearts Drove

Location Notes

An unmanned 'red and green' gated road crossing on the outskirts of Whittlesey, just into the countryside. The location is at the start/end of a banked curve, which is known as 'Whittlesea Curve'. All trains have to sound their horns here because the crossing is unprotected.

Some dog walkers will use the crossing and also some workers going to the water works. They are often friendly and always kind if you assist them in opening the gates on your side.

1) 66588 eases rounds the 'Whittlesea Curve' heading east with a Felixstowe bound intermodal.
Photo by Jonathan Benton, May, 14:30, dslr@40mm

Public Transport

National Express operates services from either Peterborough or from March and Ely.

Amenities

Whittlesey has all you will need, there are chip shops, kebab shops and plenty of newsagents.

Photographic Notes

For trains approaching from the Peterborough direction the line sweeps into the 'Whittlesea Curve' offering either a wide view of the train, or a head on curve shot with the back of the train curving round behind the loco.

The area is also, currently, well populated with semaphore signals operated from the box opposite the station. These will change, giving you a clue to the direction of the approaching working

Eastbound workings will usually be slowing for an upcoming 60mph line speed change to the east of the station.

The area is free from any noises that would interfere with audio recordings and there is plenty of room for video tripods.

2) 66724 heads west with a Doncaster bound working.
Photo by Robert Brooks, May, 14:45, dslr@40mm

Whittlesea, Hearts Drove

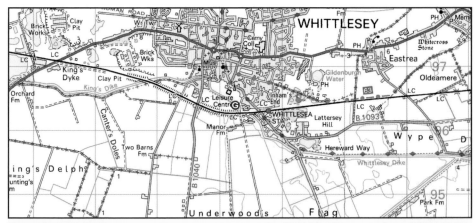

Postcode: PE7 1UH   **Lat N52:32:57**   **Long W00:07:25**

Road Directions

From the Peterborough Ring Road (A1139) leave at either junction 3a or 4, which is opposite the large Ikea distribution centre and take the A605 Peterborough Road to Whittlesey. In Whittlesey take the A1093 towards the station. Shortly before the station there is a 'Y' junction where Aliwal Road forks off to the right, take this road and follow it to the location.

You can either drive over the canal, there is a small amount of parking space here, or park before you reach the bridge.

3) 60091 heads west with an Ely to Peak Forest working. The rear of the train is in Whittlesea station.
Photo by Jonathan Benton, October, 15:00, dslr@44mm

Whittlesea, Black Bush and Ramsey Road

Location Notes
This location is some road crossings and footpaths around the rail line in flat open countryside to the east of the city of Peterborough, close to the brick works.

1) (#1) The Class 40 Preservation Society's 40145 on their 3 day 'Silver Jubilee' tour, heading east.
Photo by Albert Dawson, January, 10:00, 45mm

Public Transport.
The location is about 30 minutes walk from Whittlesea station, either through the town or along the Briggate river paths.

Amenities
There are plenty of shops, including 'West End Stores', on the High Street.

Accommodation
There is the Boat Inn, which is a guest house, on the corner of on Ramsey Road and Briggate West and there are plenty of hotels and guest houses in Peterborough.

2) (#2)A GBRf loco convoy heads east to Whitemoor.
Photo by Jon Benton, November, 10:30, 400mm

Photographic Notes
Location #1 offers a view of the railway crossing the river. Locations #2 and 3 are opposite level crossings with views east and west.
All three locations have the brickwork chimneys dominating the skyline to the west.
With the line running roughly west to east there are angles for most of the day.
Both of the crossings will give you notice of approaching workings when the barriers lower.
There is only the brickworks in the area to provide distant noise, and the crossing barriers, to interfere with audio recordings.

3) (#1) 40145 crosses Kings Dyke also heading east
Photo by Ewan Tait, January, 10:00, 50mm

Whittlesea, Black Bush and Ramsey Road

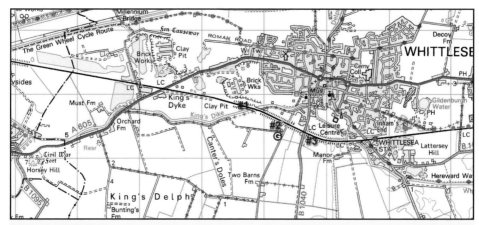

Postcode: PE7 2LH　　　　　　**Lat N52:33:07**　　　　　　**Long W00:08:15**

Road Directions

From the Peterborough Ring Road (A1139) leave at either junction 3a or 4, which is opposite the large Ikea distribution centre and take the A605 Peterborough Road continuing to Whittlsey. In Whittlesey village follow the B1040, signposted Ramsey.

After you cross a small river bridge on the edge of the village you can either continue straight along the B1040 for the Ramsey Road Location, or, immediately turn right down Briggate West to reach the Black Bush Crossing. For the bridge crossing location you should park before Black Bush Crossing and walk down the dirt track on your right.

The crossings have field entrances with spaces for a few cars.

4) With an eastbound La Farge stone, 66170 heads past the Ramsey Road (#3) crossing on its way to Broxbourne.
Photo by Brian Carter, March, 10:00, 50mm

Bury St. Edmunds Line

General Notes

The line west from Haughley Junction, at the eastern end, to Soham is double track. It singles in Soham, around the site of the former station, and continues as single track all the way to Ely Dock Junction, where it joins the Cambridge to Kings Lynn section. There is also the 16 mile single track section between Coldham Lane Junction, Cambridge, and Chippenham Junction, just past Newmarket. There is a passing loop at Dullingham Station.

1) 170204 heads east out of Ely to Bury St Edmunds.
Photo by Richard Tearle, October, 16:30, 85mm

Passenger Traffic

National Express East Anglia is the sole passenger operator. Cambridge to Ipswich workings usually produce 153s with the occasional 156, Ipswich to Peterborough traffic is dominated by 170s with 156s or 153s standing in as required.

Freight Traffic

Thre are cross country intermodals flows, continuing on from the Peterborough to Ely line, to Felixstowe. These are operated by Freightliner, GBRf and DB Schenker. Although the class 66s currenlty holds the traction monopoly, Freightliner 70s are expected to appear in 2010.

2) 66718 powers up the bank towards Thurston.
Photo by Geoff Tibble, June, 13:15, 170mm

There are also regular aggregate flows, operated by Freightliner and DB Schenker, to the region's stone terminals in Barham, Norwich, Broxbourne and Middleton Towers.

Occasional Traffic

Charter traffic is rare, but not unheard of. Test trains are also infrequent visitors. But every autumn there are the RHTT workings, out of the Stowmarket base.

3) Pathinders 20/20 Vision tour heads towards Sizewell, passing east bound through Elmswell, towards Ipswich.
Photo by John Hooson, March, 10:45, 170mm

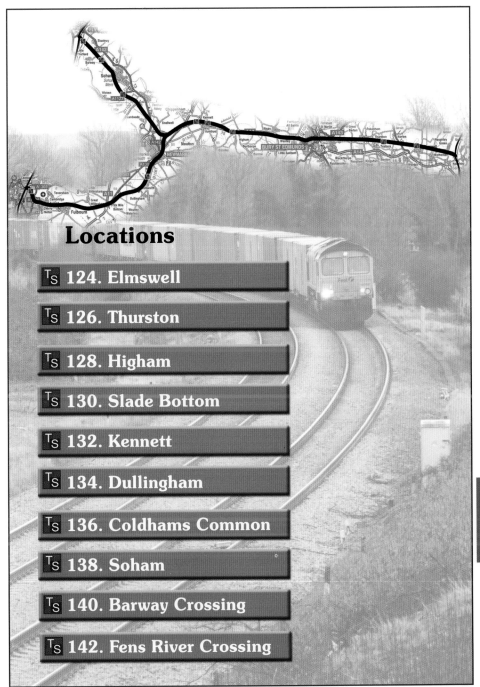

Locations

Elmswell

Location Notes

Elmswell is situated on the A14 corridor, 9 miles east of Bury St Edmunds and 7 miles west of Stowmarket. There is a railway crossing at the location. This is open farmland. The railway is on an embankment between two fields.

Public Transport

There is a frequent rail service between Ipswich and Cambridge.
Leave the the station and take Station Road south. Turn right into School Road and follow this road out of the village and follow the tree lined road towards the railway.

Amenities

There is a Chinese restaurant and a chip shop in Elmswell, situated next door to each other but they are only open from 17:00 to 22:30 Tuesday to Sunday. There is also a wide variety of shops and pubs. The main shop is the Co-op which has the Post Office just to the left. Also there is the Mace in Station Road. The two pubs are The Fox and the Railway Tavern. The Fox is next to the level crossing, and the Tavern is on School Road opposite the Fire Station.

Accommodation

There is the Elmswell Hall which is right opposite the location.

Photographic Notes

The location is best suited to shots of eastbound workings. The railway is on an embankment on a long straight. There are a few trees growing, but nothing that cannot be worked around.
For westbound workings from the crossing you have a quiite limited field of view as the railway emerges from a cutting. You could walk into the fields for a view but you would be well below the level of the railway line.

Please be aware that the grass embankments leading up to the level crossing have covered drainage ditches along their length, stick to the well trodden areas when going up or down the bank.

1) 20305 heads a westbound RHTT towards Bury.
Photo by Geoff Tibble, October, 16:00, 70mm

2) 66420 and 66426 top and tail a westbound RHTT.
Photo by Geoff Tibble, December, 15:00, 45mm

3) 66501 with a westbound intermodal.
Photo by James Welham, August, 06:45, 70mm

Elmswell

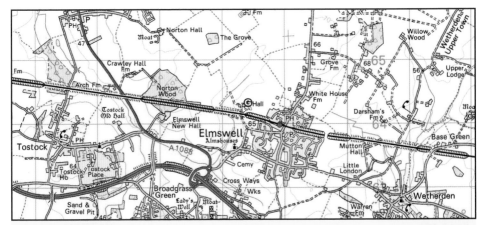

Postcode: IP30 9EN   **Lat N52:14:23**   **Long E00:54:11**

Road Directions

From the A14, leave at Junction 47 (A1088) and follow the signs to Elmswell. Elmswell Church is on your left. Immediately after the Church turn left into School Road. Then take the first turning on the left (Parnell Lane).

There are roadside verges along the approach to the location but when parking make sure you do not park too close to the railway as you will end up with your car in the shot.

4) Though the traction is long gone, the view remains. 37185 & 009 head east to Felixstowe with a 'Freightliner'.
   Photo by John Hooson, February, 10:15, 80mm

Thurston, Grimwoos Bridge

Location Notes

Thurston is a small, thriving, village a few miles east of the market town of Bury St Edmunds. The location is a position a few miles east of the station, towards the top of the steady incline that trains heading towards Bury St. Edmunds have to climb.

Situated on a single track over bridge, in the middle of the open countryside, it is a very pleasant spot. It is however, a narrow country lane and care should be taken to keep off the road.

1) With a local service bound for Ipswich, 'One' 170208 starts the descent on the line towards Stowmarket.
Photo by Geoff Tibble, June, 13:00, 300mm

Public Transport

Galloway European, services 384/385, operate almost hourly between Bury St Edmunds, Tayfen Terrace and Stowmarket Station.

You should alight at the Gardeners Arms bus stop in Tostock village and walk for about 10 minutes to reach the location.

Accommodation

There are plenty of local guest houses and hotels in Bury St Edmunds and a few near to Thurston eg Thurston Grange or Ravenwood Hall Hotel at Rougham just off the A14.

Photographic Notes

Good for photos both in directions. The sun can be head on early and late in the day but for most of the day it is on the south side, giving great shots of

2) Clearing leaves from the line 37608 tails 087 west.
Photo by Geoff Tibble, November, 09:15, 100mm

trains. There is little noise other than the ambient countryside sounds to spoil audio tracks and westbound trains will be working on the climb so it is a good location for video.

The bridge parapets are reasonably low so a step ladder will not be required. However the road only has a narrow grass strip separating the sides from the road so anyone with a tripod should take care.

Thurston, Grimwoos Bridge

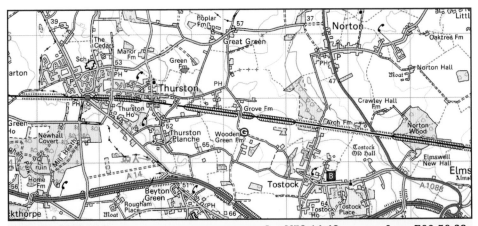

Postcode: IP31 3SG　　　　**Lat N52:14:48**　　　　**Long E00:50:39**

Road Directions

From the A14: leave at Junction 47, for Elmswell and head north on the A1088. Turn left at Church Road and continue through Tostock village. At the end of the village turn left then after about 100 yards turn right into Hollow Lane. Continue along this road for about 300 yards and turn right at the junction through the small wood. This leads to the location.

There is space for one or two cars just to the north of the bridge, but it may be better to park further down the road and walk back to the bridge.

3) GBRf 66707 and 66711 unusually provide double power for the La Farge Self Discharge train to Mountsorrel.
Photo by Geoff Tibble, November, 09:30, 135mm

Higham, Seven Mile Bridge

Location Notes

A remote rural footpath and field edge location about two miles to the west of Bury St Edmunds. The footpath crosses over the line in a shallow cutting.

1) 20312 tails an eastbound RHTT working heading back to Stowmarket..
Photo by Scott Borthwick, November, 13:30, 45mm

Public Transport

There is no practical public transport option to the location as the buses in the area are based around school run times and run only twice a day.

Amenities

There is nothing in the area, the nearest shops are in Bury St. Edmunds, where there is a full range of amenities including a Tesco store.

Photographic Notes

The field edge is better suited to eastbound shots with the curve under the A14 road bridge bringing workings sweeping round in front of you. For westbound shots from this point you will be looking over the sides of the cutting. The foot crossing is a better option for westbound shots as it has a straight approach to the location.

There is plenty of room on the field edge to set up tripods so video should be no problem. However there will be no warning of approaching trains as the A14, whilst not intrusive, will mask the sound of approaching workings.

2) 66574 heads a mostly empty intermodal west.
Photo by Albert Dawson, May, 12:15, 150mm

Higham, Seven Mile Bridge

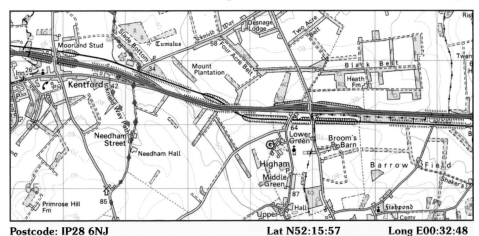

Postcode: IP28 6NJ   **Lat N52:15:57**   **Long E00:32:48**

Road Directions

Leave the A14 at Junction 40 and head south towards Higham village. Cross the road over the railway bridge and follow the road as it forks right.

Take the next left turn and park on the grass verge. Walk back to the road, turn left and the footpath to the location is about 50 yards along on the right.

3) The DRS mission to clear the leaves where no leaf has settled before, boldly carried out by 20309 and 20312.
Photo by Scott Borthwick, November, 13:30, 55mm

Kennett, Slade Bottom

Location Notes
Just to the east of Kentford and Kennett villages, this location is a shot across fields to an embankment where the line heads east to west.

1) From the A14 bank, a local working along the line with vinyled 156402 extoling the virtues of Norwich shopping.
Photo by Peter Foster, November, 15:00, 300mm

Public Transport
Leave Kennett Station and turn right down Station Road. At the end turn left and continue along Bury Road (B1506) towards the A14 following the signs to the Stud. It is about a 20 minute walk.

Amenities
There is a petrol station on Bury Road, just west of the turning to the location. Kennett village has a number of pubs. There is also a post office in Kentford that sells light snacks.

2) 66199 heads an intermodal east towards Ipswich.
Photo by Calum Hepplewhite, November, 15:00, 35mm

Photographic Notes
The line runs east to west and the shot of choice is of westbound workings, so lighting will favour afternoon shots. The shot of eastbound workings is marred by the tree line and better options exist in the area.

The noise of the A14 will feature heavily on audio soundtracks so it may not be suitable for video work. But there is plenty of room for tripods if you can live with the noise.

Kennett, Slade Bottom

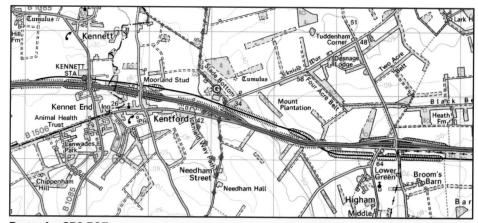

Postcode: CB8 7QT   **Lat N52:16:21**   **Long E00:31:22**

Road Directions

If you are travelling eastbound on the A14 leave at junction 40 and get back on the westbound carriageway. On the westbound carriage leave at junction 39, signed posted for Moorland Stud. Once on the slip road take the right turn, back under the A14, and there is a field entrance on your right where you can park.

3) 66728 heads towards Ely with its Hams Hall bound intermodal trailing back towards Higham.
Photo by Calum Hepplewhite, November, 14:00, 70mm

Kennett

Location Notes

The Kennett location is about half a mile south of Kennett village on the B1085. Newmarket is a few miles to the west and Bury St. Edmunds a few miles to the east. There are some houses nearby.

1) GBRf Bluebird 66708 hauls a shorter than normal train eastbound towards the station and then on to Felixstowe.
Photo by Brian Carter, month, xx:xx:, dslr@XXmm

Public Transport

The Cambridge - Ipswich trains call at Kennett, although most of the Peterborough - Ipswich ones do not.

Amenities

There is a pub in Kennet End, half a mile south on the B1085 and there is a range of facilities in Newmarket.

Photographic Notes

The line runs roughly east to west here, after curving in under the A14. Eastbound shots favour the trackside location in the field just before the beginning of the cutting into the station. Lineside vegetation can be quite high here in the summer so a step ladder will be required to gain extra height.

From the roadside you can shoot both east and westbound workings, but once again lineside vegetation can intrude.

Both locations are next to the A14 which is a busy road and traffic noise would be a major issue, but should you wish to shoot video there is plenty of space to set up a tripod.

Kennett

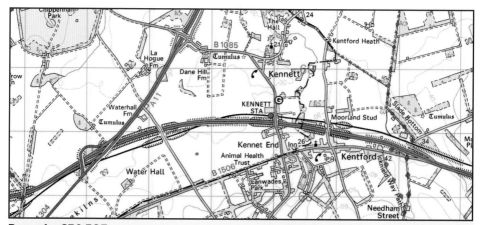

Postcode: CB8 7QF   **Lat N52:16:39**   **Long E00:28:29**

Road Directions

There is a lay-by opposite the location on the A14 eastbound carriageway but if you are planning to stay for more than a short period of time the easiest access is from the A14 (westbound). Leave the A14 at junction 39 (B1506) signed for Kentford, Kennett and the Moorland Stud. Turn right at the second crossroads onto the B1085 which leads to the station and its car park.

From the north, south or west, it is best to approach from the A11 at Red Lodge. Follow the B1085 to Kennett; the station is about half a mile after the village.

Once parked in the station car park, come back out of the station over the railway bridge and the entrance to the field is on your right, walk down the edge of the field to reach the location.

2) 66571 heads west towards Ely with and intermodal consisting mainly of 9ft 6in container pocket wagons.
Photo by Brian Carter, April, 11:30, 85mm

Dullingham, Devil's Dyke

Location Notes

Dullingham is to the west of Newmarket on the Cambridge-Newmarket line. The location is a foot crossing in open fields.

1) Slowing for a pathing stop at Dullingham, Freightliner 66594 in charge of a Felixstowe to York Holgate intermodal.
Photo by David Smith, October, 12:45, 45mm

Public Transport

There is no regular bus service that stops closer than the railway stations.

The walk from Dullingham railway station is about 2 miles. Walk south east along the road towards the village and take the first left in the village (after about ½ mile). This road leads to the B1061; turn left and after nearly a mile you reach the lay-by mentioned in the road directions - take the footpath on the left up to the railway line.

The walk from Newmarket railway station is also about 2 miles. Turn left out of the station, right at the T junction by the railway bridge, and left at the next junction with the B1061. After 1½ miles (1 mile after the level crossing) is the lay-by; take the footpath on the right up to the railway line.

Amenities

The nearest shops and food are in Newmarket, 2 miles away.

Accommodation

Newmarket has some hotels and guest houses and Cambridge is only a few miles away.

Photographic Notes

The line runs almost north to south at this point. Stand on the bank inside the gate on the south east side of the foot crossing. A step ladder may be useful to get a clear view over some of the bushes for eastbound trains.

The light is right for eastbound trains first thing in the morning, until about 09:00 if you want the sun on the nose. For westbound trains, the light is right until around midday.

Later in the afternoon the light moves round onto the other side of the crossing and a shot of westbound trains is possible, although the back of long trains will be lost behind some bushes.

The location is far from any major sources of noise so audio recordings should be clean.

Dullingham, Devil's Dyke

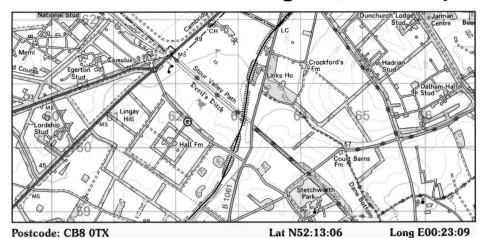

Postcode: CB8 0TX   **Lat N52:13:06**   **Long E00:23:09**

Road Directions

From Newmarket take the B1061 south west towards Dullingham and Linton. Just over a mile after the level crossing, park in the lay-by on the right hand side of the road and follow the signed footpath towards the railway.

2) A pair of DRS Choppers head towards Cambridge with a RHTT working..
Photo by Brian Carter, October, 16:00, 85mm

Cambridge, Coldhams Common

Location Notes

On the northern outskirts of Cambridge, this location is a footbridge between a park and a common, close to a residential area. Cambridge United's Abbey Stadium is just to the north.

1) Heading towards Bury St. Edumnds, 156417 powers up the 'railway avenue' towards the Barnwell Road bridge.
November, 12:45, 100mm

Public Transport

The walk from Cambridge railway station is about 1¼ miles. Go through the station car park to the far corner, by the cycle bridge, and turn right along Devonshire Road. At the end turn right on Mill Road, over the railway bridge and then third left into Sedgewick Street. Continue along its length, it becomes Cromwell Road at the vehicular width restrictions, and you eventually reach Coldhams Lane. The footbridge is visible across the common. There are bus stops on Coldhams Lane, but they do not run anywhere near the station.

Amenities

There are an Asda and Sainsbury's stores within 10 minutes walk. Other shops, including a chip shop and other take-always, are on Mill Road. There are plenty of pubs within ½-1 mile, many serving food and several listed in the CAMRA Good Beer Guide. Head towards the station or city centre for most of them.

Photographic Notes

The line runs north west to south east so the best shots are of eastbound trains, or going away shots of westbound trains, from mid to late morning until late afternoon standing.

Shots from the north side of the line earlier in the morning are not possible due to lineside bushes. In winter, beware of shadows from lineside vegetation. Use a standard lens.

For videographers there may be a little faint background traffic noise - Coldham's Lane is quite busy. The bridge itself is of lattice construction so there are no problems seeing over the sides.

Cambridge, Coldhams Common

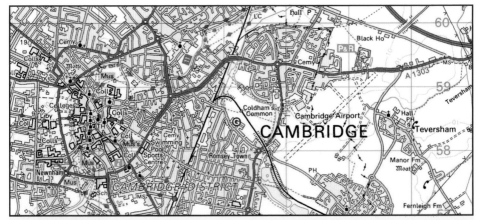

Postcode: CB1 3HZ   **Lat N52:12:22**   **Long E00:09:14**

Road Directions

From A14 Cambridge northern by-pass eastbound: Leave at junction 34 (B1047) (Fen Ditton, Horningsea) and turn right towards Cambridge and through Fen Ditton. At the traffic lights (T junction) turn right onto Barnwell Road. If westbound on the A14: Leave at the A1303 (Cambridge, Stow-cum-Quy) junction and turn left at the roundabout (1st exit) onto the A1303 towards Cambridge. After passing Cambridge airport and entering the built-up area turn left at the roundabout (1st exit) onto Barnwell Road.

From Barnwell Road immediately after the railway bridge, turn right (3rd exit) at the roundabout beside Sainsbury's into Coldham's Lane. About ½ a mile along this road Coldham's Common appears on the right. Park on the roadside spaces around here and walk across the common to the footbridge.

2) The very rare sight of AC locomotives on this stretch of line. 66541 pilots 86607 & 613 towards Dullingham.
Photo by Brian Carter, April, 12:00, 50mm

Soham, Wiken Road

Location Notes

This location is a bridge located in the middle of open fenland and is very open to the elements without any shelter. There is a farm track which leads to a public footpath running parallel to the railway.

1) 66708 powers an intermodal past Westside Farm with an Ely and on to Hams Hall working.
Photo by Geoff Tibble, December, 13:30, 200mm

Public Transport

Stagecoach, service 12, operates half hourly between Ely Station and Down Field Centre Road from where it will be a 5 to 10 minute walk to the location.

Amenities

There is a petrol station with the usual facilities about a mile up the road on the roundabout junction of this road with the A142. The nearest toilets are in Soham village pub or in Newmarket or Ely Tesco.

2) Hire in 66522 with a Felixstowe bound intermodal.
Photo by Geoff Tibble, December, 11:00, 50mm

Accommodation

There is a motel on the A142 bypass between Ely from Soham.

Photographic Notes

With the line running roughly north west to south east the sun is in a very good position from mid morning to mid afternoon from the farm track looking back to the bridge for Bury bound workings.

Shots of Ely bound trains from the bridge are better lit on late summer afternoons.

The bridge sides are not overly tall so a step ladder should not be required.

The area is free from noise, aside from passing traffic, so would suit videographers.

3) An Ipswich bound local working with 170201.
Photo by Geoff Tibble, December, 12:30, 180mm

Soham, Wiken Road

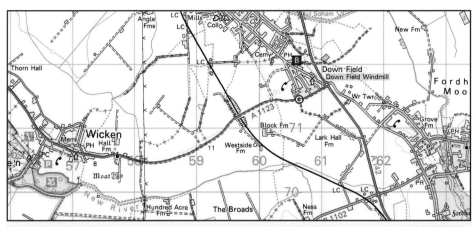

Postcode: CB7 5FY   **Lat N52:18:56**   **Long E00:20:28**

Road Directions

From the A10 in Stretham, about 3 miles south of Ely, at the roundabout take the A1123 east toward Wicken and continue through the village. The bridge is about 2 miles east of Wicken Village.

From the A14: Leave at junction 37 and travel north on the A142. After about 5 miles turn left at the roundabout onto the A1123. The bridge is about a mile along this road.

There is a private farm access track from beside the bridge and limited parking nearby on the opposite side of the road. Find a safe place to leave the car and as there is some traffic along this road take care on the narrow pavements on the bridge. There is not a lot of room to stand or walk there.

4) GBRf 66708 heads towards Ely with a Hams Hall bound intermodal seen from the A1123 bridge.
Photo by Geoff Tibble, December, 13:30, 65mm

Barway Crossing

Location Notes

Barway Crossing is in open fields. Barway village has only one road in and out. Located in the village is a large vegetable processing and packing factory, so expect large numbers of artics to thunder past. Barway also has a bus company, Leroy's A&P Travel, so expect older double deckers at school times. The only buildings are the crossing keeper's cottage and a few barns.

1) Catching the early morning rays GBRf's 66716 crosses the level crossing with an intermodal bound for Felixstowe.
Photo by Geoff Tibble, May, 08:15, 335mm

Public Transport

Stagecoach, service 12, operates hourly from Ely Railway Station to Newmarket. The stop, Soham, Eye Hill Drove is opposite Barway Road, which leads to the location.

Amenities

There is nothing at the site and Barway village has no shops at all.
The nearest facilities are in Soham and Ely.

Photographic Notes

The line runs north west to south east so the location favours eastbound workings until early afternoon, after that westbound workings from the south of the line.

The location is a gated farmers' crossing and there is plenty of room for video tripods. The line passes across the fields on a slight embankment so there is nothing to throw shadows over workings.

The location is also well away from sources of noise, other than the wind, making this an ideal location for video.

2) From the crossing side, 66535 heads east to Felixstowe.
Photo by Geoff Tibble, November, 15:30, 55mm

Barway Crossing

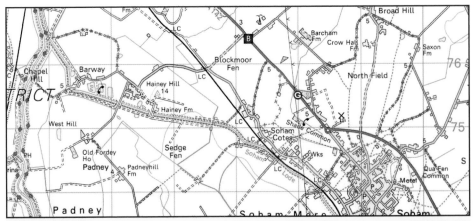

Postcode: CB7 5FY   Lat N52:18:56   Long E00:20:28

Road Directions

Take the A142 from Ely towards Newmarket. This is the road that crosses, or dives under, the line to the north of the station. After about 3 miles you will see a right turn to Barway. Take this and you will find yourself at the level crossing. The farmers' crossing is off the road that turns off just prior to the crossing. There are several lay-bys to park in. From the south leave the A14 at junction 37 and take the A142 north. Barway Road is about 10 miles on the left.

3) With a DRS entry for the 'clagging cup' 37508, with 37087, attempts an eastbound smoke screen on Ely Cathedral.
Photo by Peter Foster, November, 12:45, 195mm

Ely, Fens River Crossing

Location Notes

Just to the south east of the City of Ely this is a footpath crossing on the Fen River Way to Waterbeach. The area is just opposite some school playing fields north of the line and farm land on the south side. Just to the north of the crossing is hard standing, rather than fields, as this was used in the reconstruction of the bridge after it collapsed when the 21:19 Mountsorrel to Chelmsford La-Farge derailed, destroying the track bed of the bridge with several wagons ending up in the river. The line was closed for over 6 months whilst a new, double track sized, single track bridge, was installed.

1) With 60034 on a tour and 60048 paused in the goods loop on the stone to Peak Forest, Ely becomes 'Tug City'.
Photo by Richard Tearle, September, 13:00, 200mm

Public Transport

Ely station is served by trains from London Liverpool Street and Kings Cross as well as cross country workings from Derby, Peterborough, Ipswich and Kings Lynn.

Amenities

There is nothing in the immediate area but there is a large Tesco store opposite the railway station.

Photographic Notes

The line curves out of Ely on an embankment to gain the height over the river. It is easy to get the cathedral into the background of any shot.

There are also shots from the footpath up to the bridge looking towards the station with the cathedral in the background.

The area is free from any sources of noise but is quite exposed, so audio recordings should be unaffected.

For shots from the east of the river the closest foot crossing is back up the footpath to Ely and down the other side of the river.

2) 20304 heads east with a RHTT, from the east bank.
Photo by Brian Carter, October, 16:00, 50mm

3) 57012 hauls a tour east, towards Bury St Edmunds.
Photo by Richard Tearle, September, 16:45, 85mm

Ely, Fens River Crossing

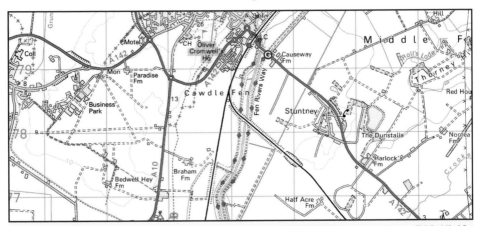

Postcode: CB7 5FA   **Lat N52:22:50**   **Long E00:15:48**

Road Directions

From the east, take the A142 into Ely. From the A10, north or south, join the A142 into Ely. In Ely continue on the A142 following the signs for Ely station. Continue past the station car park until you reach the roundabout near Tesco. Here, turn right and follow the A142 under the railway and then take the next right immediately into the playing fields entrance. You can park here and then walk back up to the road and take the footpath south to the crossing.

If you cannot park here then return into Ely and use the Tesco car park, although this does have limited time, or the station pay car park.

It used to be possible to drive down the footpath, but there is now a locked gate preventing this.

4) 66625 disturbs the very early morning Fenland mist with a diverted Barham stone working.
Photo by Geoff Tibble, May, 05:45, 50mm

Cambridge to Kings Lynn - 'Fen Line'

General Notes

This chapter also includes Ely, which is the junction of the lines from Peterborough, Kings Lynn, Norwich, Ipswich and London. Traffic on the Peterborough, Norwich and Ipswich (Bury St. Edmunds) lines is covered in their own chapters.

The line, from Cambridge, is double track until just north of Littleport where it remains single to Downham Market. The line then doubles for a few miles before reverting back to single track all the way to Kings Lynn.

Traffic heading for Middleton Towers will break off the line just prior to Kings Lynn station and head into a yard where it must reverse before accessing the 3¼ mile branch to the terminal. Although there is the loop at Queen Adelaide this is only available in one direction, clockwise, for trains that need to end up heading west towards March and on to Peterborough. Ely station is commonly used to reverse workings, Peterborough to Kings Lynn, that cannot use the loop.

2) Vinyl covered 365510 heads south towards Littleport.
Photo by Richard Tearle, October, 15:15, 85mm

Passenger Traffic

First Capital Connect operates from Kings Lynn to either London Kings Cross or London Liverpool Street, this is usually class 365 EMUs but 317s frequently appear on the line.

Freight Traffic

There is only one working to use this line and that is aggregate traffic for Middleton Towers quarry which is west of Kings Lynn. This traffic usually runs daily, although there are sometimes two trains a day depending on demand

2) 66163 approaches Queen Adelaide with the sand train.
Photo by Brian Carter, March, 09:45, 55mm

Occasional Traffic

Weekend charters are unusual on the Kings Lynn Section, but they are more common between Queen Adelaide and Ely, where they often reverse to get to Peterborough. The 'Cathedrals Express' tours often visit the city of Ely. Passing steam charters often stop for water in the yards to the south of the station.

During the autumn there is lots of RHTT activity, with Anglian workings passing through on their laps of the region.

3) The CFPS 'Silver Jubilee' passes over the Great Ouse.
Photo by Richard Tearle, January, 10:45, 30mm

Cambridge to Kings Lynn - 'Fen Line'

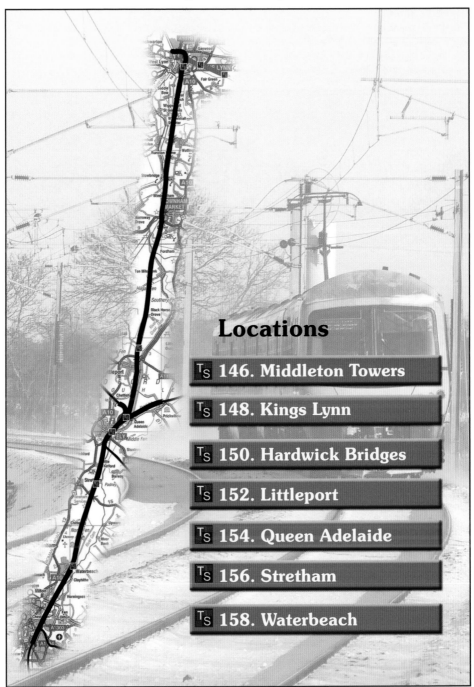

Locations

- ^T_S 146. Middleton Towers
- ^T_S 148. Kings Lynn
- ^T_S 150. Hardwick Bridges
- ^T_S 152. Littleport
- ^T_S 154. Queen Adelaide
- ^T_S 156. Stretham
- ^T_S 158. Waterbeach

Kings Lynn, Middleton Towers

Location Notes

This is open countryside with many trees lining the quarry borders. On the former route to Dereham, this is now the end to the freight only line to Sibelco quarry.

The area to the south of the line is open farmland. To the north is quarry. Given the industrial nature you will have many lorries passing and the area will generally be active during business hours.

1) 57012 arrives at the terminal's network rail boundary with a rail tour from London.
   Photo by Albert Dawson, October, 14:00, 130mm

Public Transport

Norfolk Green, service 48, operates hourly from Kings Lynn railway station to the main road, called Brow of the Hill, to the north of the location. From here it would be a 20 minute walk to the location.

Amenities

There is nothing in the immediate area, the closest facilities are in the Gaywood area of Kings Lynn.

Photographic Notes

The arrival shot is free from any major sources of shadow for a reasonable length of the train. Any working approaching will be going dead slow for the crossing and arrival.

For shots of locos in the facility you will need to walk down the field edges and through the trees to reach the end of the unloading facility.

Trains tend to have the loco at the eastern end until loading has finished and then they run round, so the shot from the crossing will only be on before the

2) 66009 progressing east through the loader.
   January, 12:00, 55mm

train departs. There are many trees along the southern edge of the line and quarry facility and these will throw shadows in bright sunlight.

Kings Lynn, Middleton Towers

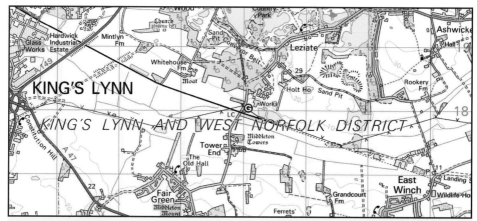

Postcode: PE32 1EQ   **Lat N52:44:01**   **Long E00:28:16**

Road Directions

From the south: At West Winch on the A10, a mile or two south of Kings Lynn turn right onto Rectory Lane, opposite the West Winch Village Stores. At the end of Rectory Lane turn left, signed 'Kings Lynn 4 miles' by an old style road sign. Then turn right on the A47 and then almost immediately left again, following the sign towards Fair Green. Pass through the village and at the end turn left into Station Road which leads to the location. From Kings Lynn take the A47 and turn left into the village of Fair Green. From Norwidh take the A47 and at the village of Middleton, turn right into Station Road.

There are a couple of field entrances that you can park in for a short while. However, if you were planning an extended stay it would better to park in the village of Leziate and then walk south to the location.

3) 60065 is ready to depart towards Kings Lynn and then run round to head south to Ely.
Photo by Brian Carter, March, 13:00, 85mm

Kings Lynn, A149 Bridge

Location Notes

The location is on the A149 Queen Elizabeth Way which is the ring road around Kings Lynn. It is quite busy, but there are wide verges on which to stand. There are very few people walking in the area.

1) From the industrial park foot bridge, west of the main location, 37612 leads 611 on a test train to Middleton Towers.
Photo by Peter Foster, November, 10:45 dslr@200mm

Public Transport

Norfolk Green, service 5, operates hourly from Kings Lynn Railway Station to Gaywood Park, Raleigh Road from where the cycle track will lead you to the footbridge location.

Amenities

There is nothing in the immediate area, but Kings Lynn has a range of shops.

Photographic Notes

The line runs roughly north west to south east here. It is more open to the east for a shot of trains having departed Middleton Towers and heading towards Kings Lynn. The prime shot is from the south of the line as there are no major obstructions along the bank. From the north side there are a few poles and a small mound of earth to work around. For trains heading towards Middleton Towers there is some lineside vegetation to deal with, making the shot quite head on. Road noise will be very intrusive here.

2) Returning from the Towers 60034 heads to Lynn.
Photo by Richard Tearle, October, 14:30, 135mm

An alternative is a footbridge to the west. This also offers a fixed distant semaphore in the shot. Located next to the Harwdick industrial units it can be quite noisy, so may not suit videographers, but does offer shots in both directions from the southern side of the bridge only. To the east there are some tall bushes in the foreground but wide or telephoto lenses should get round these.

Kings Lynn, A149 Bridge

Postcode: PE30 4LR   **Lat N52:44:16**   **Long E00:25:09**

Road Directions

Depending on your approach direction take either the A17, A141, A10, A47 into Kings Lynn which will get you to the Hardwick Roundabout. From there get onto the A149 and you will drive over the bridge after about 1½ miles.

There are a couple of lay-bys on the A149, but they are a significant walk to the road bridge.

For the footbridge, come off the A149 onto the A1076 at the Hospital Roundabout (about a mile further on) and continue into Gaywood. When you reach the traffic lights with the clock tower, Aldi and tyres depot, turn left down Queen Mary Road and follow this road round. You will pass a school on you right. Just after the school is a blue cycle path sign. Park around here and continue on foot following the cycle track, keeping close to the edge of the school, to the footbridge.

3) With the usual traffic type on the line, 60065 heads west to Kings Lynn with a rake of loaded mineral wagons.
Photo by Brian Carter, March, 13:00, 85mm

Kings Lynn, Hardwick Road Bridge

Location Notes

You are on a busy road that leads into the centre of Kings Lynn from the southern side, close to the site of the former Campbell's soup factory. Although, at the time of writing, scheduled for demolition, the distinctive Campbell's tower provides an iconic landmark directing you to the location.

1) 365533 accelerates away from Kings Lynn with a Kings Cross bound working.
   December, 11:00, 55mm

Public Transport

Norfolk Green, service 37, provides an hourly service to the Retail Park from the railway station. You need the stop after Cemetery Lodge, this is opposite the McDonald's.

Kings Lynn Railway station is served by trains from London and Ely with connections to the Midlands.

Amenities

There is a McDonald's just opposite the bridge with toilets and a range of food products. Further down the road there is a Tesco store and number of other fast food outlets usually associated with retail parks.

Photographic Notes

The line runs roughly north east to south west at this point. Most of the overhead equipment is located on the western side of the line so the only shots are to be had from the east. This makes it an interesting location for very early morning workings towards Kings Lynn or departures until early afternoon. Once the sun has moved round to the west of the line the location of the overhead masts makes shots from the west of the line unviable.

Given the amount of road traffic this would be an unsuitable location for audio recordings.

It would be easily possible to walk from either of the industrial estate bridges back to this location whilst a Middleton freight runs round in Kings Lynn yard, though a swift reversal of a top and tail working might require a more brisk walk.

Kings Lynn, Hardwick Road Bridge

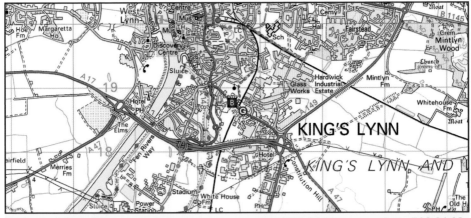

Postcode: PE30 4HR   **Lat N52:44:28**   **Long E00:24:28**

Road Directions

Approach Kings Lynn from either the A17 from the north west, A47 from the south West, A10 from the south, A47 from the south east or A148/149 from the north east and you eventually reach the Hardwick Roundabout. Exit the rounabout onto Hardwick Road, to the north west, following the signs to Kings Lynn Town Centre and heading through the retail parks. At the second set of traffic lights turn left and park, noting any parking restrictions, in the McDonald's car park.

From there walk back to the road and turn left up to the bridge.

2) 37608 and 607 slow on the approach to Kings Lynn with a touring Ilford - Derby RTC via Liverpool Street test train.
Photo by Brian Carter, Febuary, 08:45, 50mm

Littleport, Poplar Drove

Location Notes
About 3 miles north of Ely this is open farm land, opposite a small residential holding, to the north of Littleport village. Just south of the location is where the line singles from the two track section from Ely. There is not much around other than fields so the only people likely to use the crossing are farmers.

1) Having left the double track behind, 365513 races towards Kings Lynn with a service from London Kings Cross .
January, 11:00, 55mm

Public Transport
There is no useful bus service to Littleport village but the location would be about 20 minutes walk from the railway station which is served by workings from London and Ely.

Amenities
Nothing in the immediate area. There are a few small shops in Littleport village, but failing that Ely will have all the amenities you would need.

Photographic Notes
The line runs pretty much north to south here. With all the overhead line equipment on the western side of the line this will put this shot on until early afternoon, when the sun will cross to the west. The line is on a raised embankment through the fields so there is nothing to throw shadows on the subject. The northbound shot is a little tighter owing to the house on the eastern side of the line, but it is on a long straight so would favour a very early, summer, morning telephoto shot.

2) 365513 as seen with a slightly longer lens.
January, 11:00, 110mm

There are no sources of noise to interfere with audio recordings and there is a good view of approaching southbound workings making this an ideal location for videographers.

Littleport, Poplar Drove

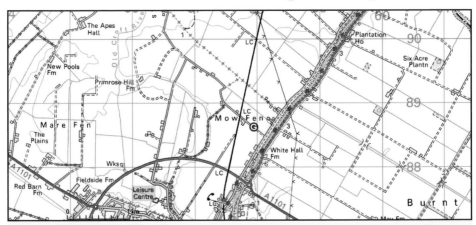

Postcode: CB6 1FB   **Lat N52:28:27**   **Long E00:19:14**

Road Directions

Take the A10 north from Ely towards Kings Lynn and Downham Market. Once you cross the railway line at Littleport take the turning on your left, Ten Mile Bank. If you miss it turn around at the roundabout just across the river and try again. Follow Ten Mile Bank north, passing all the small houses on your left and Poplar Drove is the first road turning on the left.

If you are planning anything other than a short stay it will be better to cross the line and park your car on the opposite side to avoid blocking the residence.

3) 365532 with the standard motive power for the line heads south towards Littleport and then on to Kings Cross.
January, 10:15, 55mm

Ely, Queen Adelaide

Location Notes

A small village location bisected by the main road from Ely to the outlying village of Prickwillow. To the north east of the city of Ely this is the point where the line from London diverges to Peterborough, Kings Lynn and Norwich.

Public Transport

Stagecoach, service 12, operates half hourly from Ely Station to Springhead Lane, from where it would be about a 15 minute walk, following the footpaths, to the location.

Amenities

There is nothing in the immediate area but there are plenty of food shops in Ely centre and there is the Tesco opposite the station.

Photographic Notes

There are various locations for the differing routes: The Peterborough line crossing offers curving-in shots best suited to mid afternoon workings heading towards Ely.

For the Kings Lynn line there are well lit morning options along the Fen Rivers Way footpath which is on an embankment slightly higher than the railway.

For the Norwich line there is an impressive shot with trains climbing out of Ely with the Cathedral dominating the horizon but a long telephoto lens is required for this shot. The wide shot at the crossing is spoilt' by an Overhead Line warning sign that is about 10 feet south of the crossing, although this can be worked around using careful positioning or a step ladder.

All of the locations are near crossings, some of which have warbling sirens which will continue until the train has passed.

There is also a loop so that traffic can travel directly from Peterborough to Norwich or Kings Lynn without the need for reversal in the Ely Station Yards. This loop is only available to westbound/clockwise trains (officially 'down'), but from all three lines heading into Ely North Junction. It is often used to turn engineers' trains from Whitemoor yard. There is a bridge over this line, as part of the main road and a footpath crossing which is accessed by walking down the footpath next to the Kings Lynn Line and then across the Peterborough line towards the Cathedral.

1) 158860 comes off the Peterbrough line towards Ely.
February, 16:00, 135mm

2) 60065 north, towards Kings Lynn with sand empties.
Photo by Brian Carter, March, 09:45, 85mm

3) 46115 on a special to Melton Mowbray.
Photo by Brian Carter, March, 10:15, 85mm

4) 47847 comes off the junction heading to Norwich.
May, 10:45, 135mm

Ely, Queen Adelaide

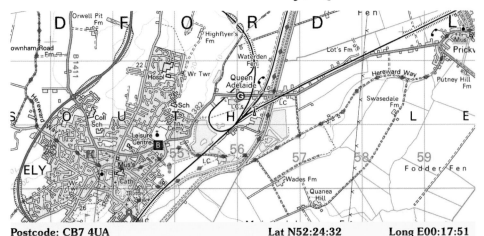

Postcode: CB7 4UA   **Lat N52:24:32**   **Long E00:17:51**

Road Directions

From the east, take the A142 into Ely. From the A10 from the south, join the A142 into Ely. In Ely continue on the A142 following the signs for Ely station. Continue past the station car park until you reach the roundabout near Tesco. Here, turn right and continue to the next roundabout and turn right under the railway line. Cross the river and then take the next left and follow this road for about 1½ miles. You will pass under the Norwich line and then at the cross roads you are in Queen Adelaide.

If approaching from the north on the A10, at the Littleport Roundabout with the A1101 continue straight across the roundabout down the road that runs parallel to the river. After several miles you will reach Queen Adelaide.

There are a number of lay-bys and side roads in the village which you can use for parking.

5) Cresting the unmistakable climb out of Ely on the way to Norwich, 67012 tops 67003 with a Serco test train.
Photo by Peter Foster, February, 09:30, 450mm

Stretham

Location Notes

This location is open fenland a few miles south of Ely City. Here the line crosses the River Great Ouse. There is a small set of moorings for river craft on the river banks to the east of the location.

1) The uniquely livered 47818 heads south with a drag from Norwich during the Ipswich tunnel blockade.
Photo by Brian Carter, January, 11:00, 85mm

Public Transport

Stagecoach, service 9, operates an hourly service between Tesco in Ely and Stretham Chapel Street from where it would be a 20 minute walk to the location.

Amenities

There are a number of small shops and a petrol station in the village, but this is more than a mile away.

Photographic Notes

The line runs roughly north to south and all shots are best suited to southbound workings as you can cross the line when the sun does.

The line is very straight and there will be plenty of notice of approaching workings. At the southern crossing there are also the barriers lowering to give extra warning. The barriers have sirens that will warble until the train has passed.

For the riverside locations there is no source of noise other than the odd passing river boat and the wind, making this suitable for videographers. The area is very exposed and wellingtons would be useful after a heavy rainfall.

2) An Advenza 57006 heads south on a scrap working.
Photo by Brian Carter, January, 11:00, 50mm

3) Cambridge bound 170395 heads south.
Photo by Richard Tearle, January, 11:00, 23mm

Stretham

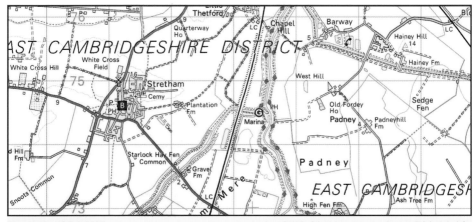

Postcode: CB6 3HR   **Lat N52:20:51**   **Long E00:14:46**

Road Directions

Stretham is on the A10 which is the main road between Cambridge and Ely.

In Stretham, at the roundabout, take the eastbound exit, the A1123, signposted to the Wicken Fen Nature Reserve and continue along this road until you reach the railway level crossing, about a mile after the village. Shortly after the crossing there is a left turn that leads to a road running parallel to the railway that heads to the marina. Take this road and after it turns away from the railway, before the marina, there is a large grass area where you can park opposite the location, but be wary as the area can get waterlogged after heavy rainfall.

4) With La Farge Aggregates PGAs from Mountsorrel, 66110 crosses the Great Ouse bound for Broxbourne.
Photo by Richard Tearle, January, 10:15, 19mm

Waterbeach, Burgess Drove

Location Notes
This location is on the western edge of the Waterbeach, about a mile north of Cambridge, on a road between fields used for grazing animals.

1) Of no interest to the horse, Cross Country 170106 heads south with a Cambridge bound working..
Photo by Brian Carter, May, 17:00, 75mm

Public Transport
The location is a short walk from Waterbeach Station. There is a footpath that runs along the eastern side of the line to the crossing.

Amenities
There are a number of small stores and a chip shop in Waterbeach.

Photographic Notes
The line is on a long sweeping curve and is well suited for afternoon southbound shots. The northbound shot, whilst clear, is not overly inspiring. You can shoot from the crossing gates or from the road. From the road a number of small trees limit the scope for shooting but not prohibitively so.
There are no major sources of noise and the area would be well suited to video, the only problems being the trees for the wide shot, or the OLE masts from the crossing gates.

2) From the western edge of the crossing, 365538.
Photo by Tom Jenkins, December, 11:00, 250mm

Waterbeach, Burgess Drove

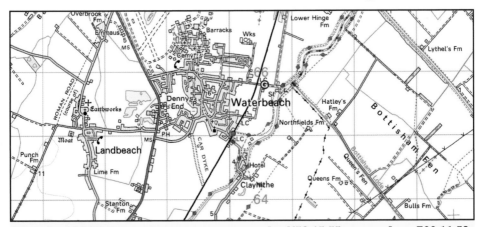

Postcode: CB25 9LL   **Lat N52:15:55**   **Long E00:11:59**

Road Directions

From the south, turn right off the A10 just before the converted pub that is now an Indian Restaurant. Stay on this road, which changes to Cambridge Road and then Chapel Street until you reach the Green.

From the north, turn left off the A10 at the traffic lights, onto Denney End Road, signposted to Waterbeach Industrial Estates and Barracks and follow the road round into Waterbeach, to the Green.

From the Green, continue towards the station but immediately after the Green, take the left turn onto St Andrews Hill. You will pass a thatched cottage on your left, take the next right, Burgess Road and continue along this road to reach the location.

There is space to park one or two cars on the roadside.

1) 66841 rounds the curve southbound with the Advenza scrap working to Hitchin.
   Photo by Brian Carter, July, 17:00, 50mm

Further Reading...

GRIDS
The Class 56 Story

Features their conception in the early 1970s to the preservation scene of today, the Mighty Grids have captured the imagination and devotion of enthusiasts nationwide. This is the complete story of their varied and unusual lives.

128 pages
200 photos, diagrams and tables
A4 Softback
Over 60,000 words
£16.95 post free

BRITS ABROAD

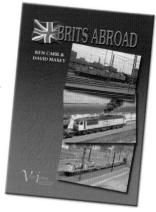

This is the first book to take an in-depth look at the diesel and electric locos that have worked on our national network and, at some point in their lives overseas as well. From the LMS shunters involved in the Second World War to the Bulgaria-bound 87s, and everything in between, this is a fascinating subject which was long overdue for serious review.

100 pages
200 photos, maps and tables
A4 Softback
Over 35,000 words
£14.95 post free

We also produce a wide range of DVDs

Full details can be found on our website...

www.visionsinternational.biz

Trainspots

The Series

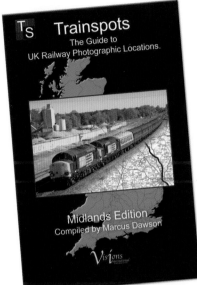

Still Available

1. Midlands

We still have a few copies left of *Trainspots* - Midlands. It features the following lines:

Birmingham - Nuneaton
Derby - Water Orton
Peterborough - Derby
Bedford - Leicester
Bedford - Bletchley
Northampton Loop
Bletchley - Birmingham
Bicester - Birmingham

Coming Soon

3. North West

The third volume of *Trainspots* covering the North West is scheduled for release in early May 2010.

Please check our website for details nearer the time.

Visions International
22 The Chase,
Boreham,
Essex CM3 3DY
tel: 01245 465974
www.visionsinternational.biz

Index

The locations in this book are listed in alphabetical order with relevant page numbers. The coloured squares refer to the coloured chapter tabs.